Faith Unraveled

A Grief Devotional for Those Struggling with Faith After Tragedy

Alisha Bozarth

 Zion Ridge Press LLC

Mt Zion Ridge Press LLC
295 Gum Springs Rd, NW
Georgetown, TN 37366

https://www.mtzionridgepress.com

ISBN 13: 978-1-955838-26-9

Published in the United States of America
Publication Date: June 1, 2022

Editor-In-Chief: Michelle Levigne
Executive Editor: Tamera Lynn Kraft

Cover art design by Tamera Lynn Kraft
Cover Art Copyright by Mt Zion Ridge Press LLC © 2022

Table of Contents

My Story:
The Day My Life Turned Upside Down

We were headed out of town. Seven days, just the two of us. Sure, it was business conventions, but it was still just the two of us. No kids, or bills, or work, or pets, or even ministry responsibilities. Our life was busy. Four kids, two businesses, two acres and a five-bedroom house. Then there was running a church including song service, preaching, and Sunday school between the two of us. Throw homeschooling in there and we had a busy mix.

Seven days with just my hubby sounded like heaven, even if I was going to be following him around two business conventions knowing about 3 percent of what they were talking about. I was the bookkeeper. I knew the finances. He knew the industry. But it would be just us. Together. For seven days. I'd take it.

We left our Bakersfield, California, home on January 5th. On that chilly winter morning we had to drive up to a nearby mountain community to drop our two daughters, Clarice and Alexi, off at the friend's home where they would be staying during our trip. My two stepsons weren't with us, living their normal lives at school and work. I drove, since my husband had just had surgery on his elbow. On a highway designed for a 65-mph speed limit, I suddenly slowed to around thirty. We hit thick fog. I hated fog. I hated it for the disorienting effect it had on me. Not that it was the densest fog I had ever seen, but it was bad. In the late morning sun, I could only see maybe fifty feet ahead of me. It was enough to put me on edge and slow me down.

My husband was in the passenger seat, chiding me for my overt and dramatic caution and anxiety. "Come on, babe. Thirty? Really?"

"I don't *like* fog."

"We have a plane to catch. Come on."

"Well, then you drive."

"Fine. Pull over."

So I did. I pulled over on the side of the freeway, a little irritated with my spouse, and we awkwardly switched seats. I was huffed at his annoying reprimand as if I was a little granny making a mountain out of a molehill. He was huffed at my "unnecessary" nerves that were going to make us late. Once we were repositioned, he eased out onto the freeway, his one good arm on the wheel.

From the passenger seat, I watched his speed. Twenty. Thirty. Thirty-five. Forty. When he hit the fifties, I squirmed. I didn't like it. But like a good wife, I kept my mouth shut. He didn't want me nagging. He was an extremely capable driver and apparently trusted his vision and reflexes.

Be quiet, Alisha. Keep your mouth shut. Don't start your trip with a fight.

It probably wasn't but five minutes after he took the wheel when it happened. We could see in the cloudy, white air, a semi-truck ahead of us in the lane. And in one second, all too late, we realized it wasn't moving. The lane to the right was also coming to a standstill. To our left were concrete barriers that took up residence in the shoulder that normally would have given plenty of room to pull over.

There was nowhere to veer.

As soon as I saw it, he of course did, too. He slammed the brakes. But it only took a second to realize we weren't going stop in time. A collision was inevitable. And even with the brakes, the collision would be with a decent amount of speed. In the last half a second, he swerved, aiming the van between the two lanes of traffic.

It's amazing how many thoughts can catapult through your mind in half a second. In that moment, not only was I bracing for impact, I was mentally questioning what in the world my husband was doing. *Why are you swerving? There's not room between the lanes. You won't fit. What's the purpose of—*

Blackness...

When I came to, the first thing I noticed was the roof of our van was torn open. Open sky was above me in the passenger seat. I looked around. My husband was unconscious in the driver's seat. The steering wheel had come forward a good foot. A huge gash cut across his leg. Other than that, he didn't look too bad.

I looked back at our daughters in the seats behind us, both also unconscious. The roof that had torn off on my side was pressed back with the impact, crunched and compacted, forming a 'v' shape, pointing down over Alexi, my younger daughter, behind the driver's seat, pinning her head down toward her lap.

My older daughter, Clarice, behind me in the passenger side, woke up next. After taking in the situation, she immediately started whimpering and crying. As I tried to comfort her, I pulled my phone out and called 911. All I could think at the moment was, *This is going to ruin our trip! We won't get this all handled and still make our plane. This is crazy! And so inconvenient!*

Little did I realize.

As I was on the phone with 911, people in the stopped traffic started coming. Alexi woke up, screaming blood-curdling cries. Her head was pinned by the roof of the van, rendering her unable to move.

Men around set out to lift the roof to unpin her. While that was going on, I was still talking to 911. When my attention was back on my husband, limp and still unconscious in the driver's seat, I realized his breathing was becoming labored. My stomach turned. I knew something was not right. The initial looks, simply unconscious with a deep cut in his leg, were deceptive. He was not okay.

At this point, I started freaking out, not over our ruined trip, but over the fact that we were thirty minutes from town, on a freeway with two accidents, and bumper to bumper traffic, in the midst of dense fog.

The ambulance would not get there in time to help.

The roof was finally off. I realized then, not only had it been pinning Alexi, it had rammed her head. Blood was all over her, dripping a pool into her lap. As people worked on her, I realized my husband's breathing was becoming even more labored — with more time elapsing between each one. But no one was helping him, only my daughter.

Maybe I'm a horrible mother, but all I could think at that moment was, *Do something for my husband.* I could handle loss as long as I had my husband by my side. I didn't think I could handle the loss of my husband.

I handed the phone to one of the men helping, who at some point revealed he volunteered or worked at the fire department. (I don't remember which specifically.) I started doing CPR on my husband myself. At that point, blood was starting to pool in his mouth, spreading onto my face as I tried desperately to borrow time until the EMT's got there. I heard the man on the phone talking with the 911 operator. I heard the words, "one viable." I struggled to absorb those words, fighting what I knew it insinuated. Only one of the two injured was likely to live.

No. He can't die. This can't be happening. It's not true. That guy doesn't know what he's talking about.

Clarice, who like me wasn't hurt, had already been ushered out of the van and pulled aside to prevent her watching the unfolding scene. I hadn't even realized that at the time, so absorbed was I in the battle before me. The men got Alexi out of the van. She was screaming uncontrollably.

Fire trucks finally arrived. As I was still trying CPR on my husband, a fireman tapped me on the shoulder. "Can I take over?"

I nodded and backed out of the van. *Yes, please. Do more than I can. Save him.* A little part of me thought it would all be okay now. *They're here. They'll know what to do.*

I turned my attention to my youngest. Someone had grabbed a blanket out of our packed things in the back and had her on the ground. I bent over her, speaking into her ear, trying to calm her over her screams. But she didn't stop. She couldn't hear me. The ambulance arrived and she was surrendered to their capable hands.

But when I glanced back to see the status of my husband inside the van, I felt my heart stop beating. My husband's body was ... covered. You know ... *covered.* The fireman! What was he doing? No! Why aren't they helping him? How could they stop?

At this point I was in a daze. Shock had frozen me. I didn't know what to do, where to go, what to think or the next course of action. And then, like a bolt of lightning, I realized I didn't know where Clarice was. I looked around frantically. Someone pointed out that she was taken off to the side and was with an elderly couple at their car. God bless strangers. I started heading that direction.

Someone stopped me. They pointed to my face. "You may want to clean the blood off your face."

Oh, yeah. I nodded dumbly. Dazed. Numb. I cleaned my face, I don't even remember with what—probably the sweatshirt I had on, it was already covered anyway—and went to find her.

I can still remember her face when she asked the question. "How's Daddy?"

At that moment I started crying. I shook my head, fighting the words. Fighting the truth. "He's gone, baby."

She stepped back, shaking her head. "No." Her face crumpled and warped. "No, no, no."

We collided in a hug, crying, trying to take in what had transpired in the last fifteen minutes.

The ambulance came and told me Alexi was being taken to the hospital. *Do you want to come?* Well of course I was going to come! Then I found out it was so serious they wouldn't let me ride in the back with her. It was then that a new reality hit me.

There was only room in the ambulance for one.

Do I go with my youngest to the hospital and leave my oldest there with strangers? The older couple assured me they would get her to us at the hospital. *Or do I stay with my oldest and chance being needed at the hospital with my youngest?* What if she woke up without me? What if a major decision needed to be made?

How do I choose?

How badly I wished my husband was there so each of us could take care of a child. But I was alone. Facing it *all*, alone.

Whether right or wrong, in my paralyzed state, I chose to go in the ambulance. I found out later, thankfully, that they took Clarice in another ambulance also, just to have her checked out. She didn't have to depend on random strangers. But, poor baby, she was left to face that ride on her own. I still feel guilty over it.

At the local hospital, they checked out each of my children. On the way, I had made several phone calls, alerting family members, including my two stepsons. I can imagine how they felt when they answered their phones, having their normal day, to hear my crying on the other end, telling them their dad was dead. And my mother-in-law? Dear Jesus. I can still remember the conversation with my mom.: "What's wrong?"

"We were in an accident."

"Is everyone okay?"

"No. No, I ... I think Kyle's gone." My voice was gnarled and muffled.

"Gone? What do you mean gone?"

"He's *gone*." (I couldn't quite bring myself to say *dead*. My brain fought against that reality. I mean, sure, I saw his body covered. But no one had *told* me he was dead. I hadn't *seen* the dead body. My mind argued for proof. Until then, I grasped the tiniest bit of hope that my assumptions were wrong.)

By the time we arrived at the hospital, family and friends had already gathered in the waiting room. News traveled fast. I cried then. Cried a lot. Cried as I was passed from embrace to embrace. Cried because I felt the wall-breaking power of people's concern. Cried because, well, I needed to break.

I don't really remember when it dawned on me, but at some point, it did—why my husband swerved at the last minute—that last moment when I was questioning his movement in my mind. In that moment, when he knew he couldn't avoid the collision, he swerved to take the brunt of the impact on himself. He swerved so that the driver's side—his side—took the hit. I walked away without a scratch. I didn't even have whiplash. There was a small bruise on my chest from the seatbelt, but that was it. My husband, however, died from blunt force trauma and internal bleeding. He took the hit. All of it he could, at least.

There were such mixed emotions. Part of me knew if he just hadn't been driving so fast, it probably wouldn't have happened. Then the other part of me crumbled, knowing he gave his life to protect his family the best he could.

I was told that my husband's body wasn't brought to the hospital. It was taken to the morgue. In my mind, I still argued that reality. Then I was informed Alexi's injuries were extremely serious. The roof had crushed her skull and she needed brain surgery. She had a severe brain bleed and needed to be flown to the children's hospital a couple hours away. But with the storm outside, they opted to drive her in an ambulance. Time was of the essence.

I didn't even have time to absorb the shock of all the events snowballing around me. Responsibility called my name. My daughter needed me. I had to go home, pack and get ready to head north to Valley Children's Hospital in Madera for an undetermined amount of time, with an undetermined outcome.

The moment I entered my bedroom, I broke down again. My husband's things still hung in the closet. His dirty shirt that said, "Thy will be done," still lay on the bed for him to use again. His presence was everywhere. My body and mind rejected my new reality. I remember grabbing a pillow and beating it against the bed. Over and over. Feeling the reverberations pound through my arms gave release to the volcano.

Then I crumpled to the floor. How had the day turned out so drastically different than planned? We should have been on the plane, landing in Minneapolis, talking about the negative five-degree weather, shuttling to our hotel and getting ready for the convention. Our girls should be with our family friend, cutting and tying the fleece blanket sets we bought for them to do.

Instead, my husband was in the morgue, my daughter's life was hanging in the balance, and I was left in the aftermath of a hurricane, figuring out how to recoup from the massive damage.

My sisters and mother went with me and my brother-in-law drove us. It was a hard thing to get back into a vehicle that night. I was exhausted, emotionally spent, and so overwhelmed. It was dark and the storm sent hard rain. During the two-hour drive, I sat in the back seat, fighting anxiety to be back in a vehicle during bad weather, and fighting emotional upheaval.

We finally arrived and sat in a waiting room for hours. By that time, it was late. I think we finally got news at 2a.m. I remember waiting, bent over with my head in my lap, drifting into restless sleep, I was so exhausted. But Alexi's surgery went well. The next time I saw my daughter, her long thick hair had been shaved off on one side, tubes were everywhere, and she had a black eye on one side. She looked awful. Delicate. Fragile. Broken.

We spent two weeks at the hospital. During that time, it wasn't just Alexi's recovery that I struggled dealing with. The whole time, I fought against the truth. Even two weeks later, I waited to get a call saying they made a mistake and my husband was alive. I had dreams—more like nightmares—of him waking up in a refrigerated morgue cell, banging to get out and no one being there to let him out. He would die! Not because he was already dead, but because they had dismissed him as dead and left him in a freezer.

I also had to figure out our business. Remember, I did the books. I had no idea how to run this business on my own. It had to shut down because of licensing issues. Finances quickly snowballed into another burden of massive debt left on my lone shoulders. My older daughter, Clarice, torn with grief and the adolescent view that her recovering sister was getting all the attention, bottled up her emotions and pulled herself away from everyone. The effects lasted for years.

And I was left to handle it all. Alone.

Life itself pressed like a massive weight. It hurt to breathe. Life looked like a mountain too high to climb. I simply wanted to go to sleep and not wake up. Not have to climb this insurmountable beast. The effort to overcome the path of destruction before me just seemed too much. Too hard. Too impossible.

It was the first time in my life I experienced a close personal loss, and it was the closest person in the world to me. My husband. We were best friends, business partners, ministry partners, workout partners, and lovers. We did everything together. As I sat in the hospital for fourteen days, trying to make sense of the collateral damage, he wasn't there to turn to. He wasn't there to make plans with. Dealing with life felt like a massive wave of blows. *Boom, boom, boom.* And ones I had to handle by myself.

I was blessed to have my parents and sisters with me every step of the way. They set aside their lives, jobs, and families to sit beside me and help any way they could. I am forever thankful they were there. They stayed in the hospital room when I needed a break. They talked to doctors when I couldn't absorb the information. They took my daughter to therapy when I needed to drive the two hours back into Bakersfield to deal with business matters. My dad stayed at my house, watching the property and animals and Clarice. He even took over the church that was now without a pastor. (My husband had been the pastor.)

But as a Christian, and one in ministry for sixteen years, I felt my faith unravel. Like a ball of yarn, I found myself strewn all over, listless and limp. I found myself completely disconnected emotionally from everything I had always believed. Even though we never taught nor believed the 'prosperity' gospel, nor that our faith excluded us from trials, I still somehow couldn't believe that this was God's will. What in the *world* would He accomplish by this? My husband had always been a shameless and outspoken believer. A pastor who passionately shared the gospel and ministered to broken lives. Why would God do this?

And here's another honest confession. The thought of honoring God felt like a burden. *A burden.* For God to receive glory in my tribulation, I felt I had to be strong, I had to be gracious, I had to be full of faith, I had to be put together. All that expectation was heavy. How could I honor God when I felt the way I did? The *opposite* of all that.

I felt pain. I felt confusion. I felt fear. I felt bitterness.

But loyalty and faith, courage and trust? Those feelings shut down. We always hear phrases like, *God allows tragedy to pull us closer to Him.* Well, it wasn't working on me. I pulled away. I retreated. I wouldn't say I lost my faith, but I questioned everything about it. I wouldn't say I turned away from my faith, but I became mentally and emotionally severed from it.

And as one who had been a pastor's kid, been in active ministry for years and stood beside my husband in various ministries, I had always felt myself to be a firm, strong believer. After that day, I felt everything but. And for years afterward.

After losing him, the spiritual things people would say ruffled my feathers. And that is putting it mildly. Their trite, soothing, or faith-filled comments made my hackles rise. On the inside, of course. On the outside, I smiled and nodded, hugged and agreed.

For months I struggled with my faith, trying to reconcile what I *knew* with what I *felt*. The fact that I struggled made me feel like maybe I was never a strong Christian to begin with. I mean, a mature Christian wouldn't crumble like that, right? I doubted myself and questioned what I believed. Maybe I was a hypocrite. Maybe I didn't really believe anything I claimed I did. Shame and embarrassment coiled inside me. I put on the smile and I quietly continued the things I had always done, going through the motions of Christianity. Partly it was my comfort zone. Partly it was pride. Partly it was the wisdom of knowing I needed to cling to it regardless. I remember feeling such a burden to face this grief thing with integrity, graciousness, strength, and faithfulness that people expected. That I expected.

I remember at one point buying the book, *A Grief Observed*, by C.S. Lewis. I craved—I *needed*—something I could relate to. I needed something from a strong, intelligent believer that showed the struggle I was in, to feel understood. Knowing someone like C.S. Lewis dealt with depression and apathy during grief helped me feel not so isolated. Not so crazy. Not so weak and horrible.

I don't even remember how or when or why it happened. But one day I had a light bulb moment, and it brought a measure of clarity. All the craziness I was feeling—did it really mean my faith was substandard? Nonexistent? Hypocritical? Weak?

Maybe it just meant I was hurting.

Once that truth hit, my mind was able to expand to more truths. But truths we don't talk about enough in the Christian circles. The truths we don't tend to be raw, honest, and open about in the church, which hinders vulnerability and transparency. In our quest to impute courage and faith into the people of God, we forget to impute the knowledge that seasons of extreme lows are also part of the Christian life. I'd even say a *normal* part of a Christian's life. Seasons of faithful men, breaking, seasons of fearless men, cowering, seasons of passionate men, retreating, are part of our human existence. And the Bible proves it. In our desire to see the people of God embrace faith and victory, obedience and zeal, I began wondering if the church prepares them to endure these deep lows and impute the correct knowledge that God loves the faith-filled, but He is also the rescuer of the faith-broken.

Once these truths started penetrating, the shame, embarrassment, and doubt lost their monopoly of control. That's not to say I stopped struggling. Oh, no, no, no, no. Healing is a long road. A slow road. There were many times when apathy, anger, restlessness, and confusion still ruled the day. But the hopelessness left. Now I felt that anchor, clutching the knowledge that down the road, I would at some point be better.

I realized my faith simply needed to heal—just like the rest of me.

But during this journey of processing what was happening inside me and digging for healing, there was something in me that wanted to be validated and not coddled. I wanted to be blunt and not proper, raw and not polished. I didn't want someone to hug me and pray for me. (Well, I did, but...) I wanted someone who would pound the ground with me. I didn't want someone who would remind me of God's goodness again. I wanted someone who would vocalize their confusion with me. I didn't want someone to smile at me. I wanted someone to scream with me.

Finally, I realized that the Bible *has all that*. We just don't talk about it much. It doesn't just have, "He heals the broken hearted," but it also has, "I cry by day, but you do not answer, and by night, but I find no rest." (Ps. 22:2)

More than anything, I realized I wasn't the only one struggling with these things. The one who didn't want the trite, calming, soothing pat on the back or another quote on how God works all things for good. But the one who begged and ached for the raw, open wound of my grief and faith, which was one wound, intertwined, unable to be separated from the other, to be seen, acknowledged, validated, and, finally, bandaged.

I wanted to heal by someone reminding me that even the bitterness I felt was normal, that the detachment I struggled with wasn't making me broken, and everything severed inside me could be healed. I wanted to heal, not by someone proclaiming the exact opposite of what I felt, but by expressing the exact thing I felt.

I wanted someone to remind me that the Bible isn't just full of faith and victory and joy, but full of anguish and doubt and bitterness.

And those Scriptures ... yes those ... are what would jumpstart my healing.

And hopefully, those are the Scriptures that will jumpstart your healing, too.

I hope the following devotional entries bless you and encourage you in this dark road of grief. It builds, ever slowly, an arc of hope that I pray will uplift and, yes, even challenge you in this hard time.

Though the entries are written as daily devotions, please feel free to do them however quickly or slowly works best for you to really process the truths presented. Use the journal pages to vent or write what the Lord speaks to you and let the Spirit minister to the deep places in ways only He can.

Big hugs, everyone.

Day One:
The Lord Hears

I am weary with my moaning; every night I flood my bed with tears; I drench my couch with my weeping. My eye wastes away because of grief. Psalm 6:6-7

Does any of that sound familiar? If God saves our tears, He had buckets of mine. I remember being so tired of grief, wishing it was like a jacket I could just strip off when it was too hot and be done with it!

David was called a man after God's heart. We picture him as a warrior who defeated Goliath. A psalmist who praised God with his many songs. A man who reigned as king of Israel for forty years. A mighty man of God and of faith.

But flooding his bed with tears? Drenching his couch? Those aren't the images that come to mind as much.

But, boy, do I understand these reactions well. I remember many nights (and days too!) when I wept so much, I wasn't sure how my body was still hydrated.

I read the verse above and think, this was the same guy who faced Goliath? The same guy who God gave the precious label, "a man after my own heart"? This is the same guy who held himself together with such integrity and principle in the face of a jealous king seeking to take his life?

Yep. The same guy.

If all you look at is David's defeat of Goliath or his passionate praise and dancing as he celebrated the Ark of the Covenant being brought into Jerusalem, or his victorious ascension to the throne, you miss the whole picture.

David was a man familiar with pain, heartaches, betrayals, and loss. He struggled and hurt. He questioned, vented, and mourned.

If you are struggling with your faith today, you are in good company. It is great to hear sermons on the people with unwavering faith in the Bible, the brilliant victories and the supernatural interventions that God wrought in people's lives. But sometimes, you just need to know that even the greats—fell. Not just a clumsy stumble of the feet, but a collision with hard ground. Sometimes you just need to hear their anguished cries, their questioning, their frustration, and know you are not the only one. Sometimes you need to see the verses that portray the dark place you are in and realize it isn't all that abnormal.

The church sometimes gets confused on what faith looks like. *If I had faith in God's sovereignty, I wouldn't be struggling so much. If I trusted God's purpose, I wouldn't be so sad.*

David is a prime example. He loved God so much that God promised him an eternal kingdom. He had so much faith in God's power and faithfulness, he faced a seasoned warrior three times his size—with no war experience—and won! He held unwaveringly to God's promise in the face of hardship, exile and persecution.

And ... he flooded his bed with tears. He teetered on the edge of despair. His soul languished in his trouble.

If you are struggling with your faith right now, don't lose heart. Don't be convinced that this dark season defines you. Don't think that you are subpar for wavering. Don't think the doubts have the power to unravel God's faithfulness.

David reminded himself of this simple and profound truth in the verse that follows the one above. "The Lord has heard the sound of my weeping. For the Lord has heard my plea; the Lord accepts my prayer." (Ps. 6:8-9) In Psalm 55:17, David says, "Every evening and morning and at noon I utter my complaint and moan, and he hears my voice."

If you ever wondered if God hears your screams, if He knows your anguish, if He cares about your misery, read those verses again.

And again.

And again.

And again.

Journal

Day Two:
Hopelessness Can Feel All-Consuming

Oh that my vexation were weighed, and all my calamity laid in the balances! For then it would be heavier than the sand of the sea. Job 6:2-3

Wouldn't it be nice to put your pain into tangible form, into some mass you could see and measure? Then maybe you wouldn't feel so crazy. You would feel justified! If you could physically lay your pain on a scale for the eye to see, it would validate your anguish.

Job basically said the same thing in the verse above. He said his pain would be heavier than the sand of the sea. What would you compare yours to?

Job endured heavy tragedy. He lost not one, not two, but ten children. Then he lost his livelihood and his health and was left in extreme physical pain. When I read some of his comments, my soul leaps in understanding. He was *brutally* honest in his struggle, and it spilled over into the things he said. Do you feel the freedom to express yourself? Even the anger? The questions? The confusion?

Job did. At one point he said, "For the arrows of the Almighty are in me; my spirit drinks their poison." Yikes. He didn't hesitate to say he felt God had crushed him. He even went on to ask God to just finish his life, it was so excruciating. (Verses 8-9) Have you ever thought that? *God just take me, because I don't want to live in this misery.* Then do you feel guilty or ashamed for being so hopeless and depressed?

Job said these things out loud. And he was a man God Himself called blameless and upright. (Job 1:8) This righteous man of God had these vexing and contrary feelings. Don't feel you are the only one to feel so mixed-up inside.

17

Have you ever thought, *I'm not strong enough for this?* If you are like me—you think it a lot. You look at God and think, *I can't. I can't do this.* Job put it this way, "Is my strength the strength of stones, or is my flesh bronze?" (Verse 12) Like, come on, Lord, I'm not made of stone to be able to carry this burden. I am pottery. Fragile and broken. Empty and shattered.

Job's words resonate with many. His suffering shows us that even the righteous and faithful feel overburdened by the pain of tragedy and loss.

You aren't alone. You aren't strange. You aren't going crazy. You aren't the only one to question. You aren't the only one who doesn't understand. You aren't the only one considering giving up and experiencing guilt for feeling that way. You aren't the only one who feels their faith is numb, unable to offer the solace it should.

Grief makes you feel practically every emotion mankind can feel—usually at the same time. No wonder it's overwhelming. No wonder we want an escape.

But ... healing does come. Healing will come. In the meantime, cry out to God.

Honestly. Bluntly. Unashamedly. Completely.

Job did.

And I'm pretty sure God could handle it.

Journal

Day Three:
The "Fluffy" Scriptures

My God, my God, why have you forsaken me? Why are you so far from saving me, from the words of my groaning? Psalm 22:1

Maybe you have had a day when you couldn't stop crying. You were struggling. Depressed. Angry. Someone came along and quoted a scripture like Psalm 34:18, "The Lord is near to the brokenhearted." And then they said something like, "Just lean on Him and let Him comfort you."

Maybe the comment made you squirm. Maybe it made you mad. Maybe it made you feel even more depressed. *What's wrong with me,* you thought, *when Scripture doesn't comfort my soul? When I feel so far away from God?*

David wrote the tranquil, encouraging words in Psalm 34, but he also wrote Psalm 22 above. Read it again. David went on in verse 2 of this Psalm to say, "O my God, I cry by day, but you do not answer, and by night, but I find no rest."

Well, that doesn't feel quite as cozy, does it?

Unfortunately, we can often relate to this verse instead of the calming words of Psalm 34. When God has allowed an earthquake into our life, causing destruction and pain, without an obvious sign of His hand bringing some type of rescue, we feel forsaken — as if He has left us in this broken condition and we have to fend for ourselves.

It's an easy thing for people to say, "Give God your pain, cast your burdens on the Lord." People say these nice-sounding things — these promises of Scripture — because they're true. But it doesn't always *feel* so simple.

Sometimes these "fluffy" Scriptures can discourage us more because we wonder why they're not working. We wonder why we're so broken that Scripture doesn't seem to help us. We wonder why God is so far away that His promises don't reach us.

David wrote the "fluffy" Scriptures in Psalm 34, but he also wrote the desperate words in Psalm 22. He had cried out to God but felt no help, felt no release, felt no relief.

God's promise isn't complicated.

But our human condition is.

Grief is messy. Our emotions are massive webs with gluey fingers that adhere to our souls and aren't easily shaken. Our weaknesses are currents pushing against God's tides of truth.

We are but dust, remember.

So, if those "fluffy" verses produce a not-so-great reaction inside you, don't worry. Your hackles don't change the truth of those verses, nor their power. It doesn't mean you're a terrible Christian. It just means you're human, you're struggling, and you're craving validation.

One day, when the waves and webs lose their strength, your feet will land back on that steady foundation and you will see it was there all along.

The best reminder is that God doesn't get tired of our groaning. He doesn't get motion sickness from our rollercoaster of emotions. He will ride the waves with us until we are out of that dark place.

So, next time someone says something too "fluffy" for you, and you feel the defensive walls rising, maybe turn to one of these darker verses and remember David's honest cries. Use them until, one day, those fluffy verses don't feel so empty anymore because the fluff has regained its comfort and substance.

One day.

Journal

Day Four:
Our Depressed Heart

And he said, "Go out and stand on the mount before the
LORD." And behold, the LORD passed by, and a great and strong
wind tore the mountains ... but the LORD was not in the wind.
And after the wind an earthquake, but the LORD was not in the
earthquake. And after the earthquake a fire, but the LORD was
not in the fire. And after the fire the sound of a low whisper. And
when Elijah heard it, he wrapped his face in his cloak. 1 Kings
19:11-13

Elijah had some awesome victories. He went toe to toe with
850 prophets of a false god. By himself. He had guts. He knew
who his God was. He knew God's power intimately.

And even with such guts, he ran away from the threat of an
evil queen like a scared puppy. Isn't it interesting that after such
a fantastic physical and spiritual victory, he slumped in defeat?

Isn't that just like us humans? Often the highs are followed
by the deepest lows: The Crash. After running away, Elijah sat
under a broom tree—alone—and asked God to take his life. He
was tired of it all. Tired of the pain. Tired of the fight. Tired of the
effort. Sound familiar?

Even the greatest of prophets can sink into depression. That
comforted me when I felt like such a failure of a Christian. Elijah
just delivered one of *the biggest victories in all the Bible.* God
withheld rain for three years at Elijah's word. He had just seen fire
fall from heaven, for goodness' sake. And yet, here he is, sitting
alone, afraid for his life, begging for God to take him.

Giving up.

Even the spiritual greats ... fall. Fall into sin, fall into
depression, fall into doubts.

If you have fallen, too, take heart. Grief often takes you down

25

one of these roads, if not all three.

And as Elijah is crying out to God, God moves. Verses 11-13 above describe how God sent a strong wind, an earthquake, a fire. But it wasn't until the whisper that Elijah felt the Lord.

There is something profound and remarkably intimate in how God chose to show Himself to Elijah. Elijah knew the Lord's might and power. He was all too familiar with His authority and supremacy. But that soft whisper is what got to him. It brought Elijah to his knees. Because the softness met him right where he was, in his desperate frame of mind.

God is ever gracious and usually shows Himself in the small things when we are struggling, rather than the big. When we feel down, depressed, or broken, God rarely shows off in bold, loud ways. As humans, I don't think we could handle the fireworks of His might.

Often, it's that still, soft, gentle voice in which God woos us back. A gentle rain that doesn't douse us all at once, but seeps softly through the hardened layers of our heart and penetrates with a slow and steady power.

Are you looking for God in those gentle ways? Can you feel Him whispering?

I wonder what God whispered to Elijah. His name? A specific word? A promise? A reminder?

What is God whispering to your broken heart?

Journal

Day Five:
Bitter Tears

> *My soul is bereft of peace; I have forgotten what happiness is. Lamentations. 3:17*

This verse ... Isn't it relatable? I marvel at how understandable this statement is. The bitterness of grief makes my soul squirm and chafe. My soul tosses and turns like my body does during a bad night's sleep because this new, unwanted life is so hard to bear. Peace seems as fanciful as a unicorn. Happiness? What is that? How can I ever be happy again?

Of all the people we might expect to hear talk in such a depressing and hopeless manner, it probably isn't a prophet of God. Yet that's whose words these are—Jeremiah's—one of the Bible's major prophets. Jeremiah wrote the book of Lamentations in the Bible. He is known as the weeping prophet. Although his grief was not a specific loss like many of ours, he still was extremely honest and open about his sadness.

In verse 4 he says, "He [God] has made my flesh and my skin waste away ... he has besieged and enveloped me with bitterness and tribulation." Do you see how honest Jeremiah was about his misery? Why do we feel the need to tuck ours away? Hide it? Deny it? Like a cat spitting up a hairball, he just vomited out all his frustration. He didn't tiptoe around it. That honesty feels good. It lets the infection out. Being strong can be exhausting. As I observe these "mighty" men of God, I never see God reject them in their desperation. I never see God rebuking them for their anger or depression.

Jeremiah goes on to say, "My soul continually remembers (my affliction) and is bowed down within me" (verses 19-20). *Bowed down within me.* This isn't someone bowing in reverence or worship, but someone so distraught that they have buckled under

29

the weight of suffering. His afflictions are constantly on his mind. His response? His soul collapses. He is spent. Weak. Do you feel that way? Join the club, there's plenty of room at the table for us weak folk. We can hang out with the likes of David and Job and Jeremiah and Elijah.

But pay attention to the very next thing Jeremiah says. "But this I call to mind, and therefore I have hope: The steadfast love of the Lord never ceases." In Jeremiah's time of vexation and anguish, pain and sadness, all he could conclude was ... God's love never ends. God's faithfulness endures.

Unfortunately, God doesn't prevent all the heartache of this world. And if He prevented Christians from experiencing heartaches, no one would serve Him for any other reason. Faith would be self-serving.

We are left in a world of tragedy and grief, with no exemption. But God isn't done. Right now, that may not comfort you. That concept didn't comfort me at first. You may not be where Jeremiah was to take hope in God's faithfulness and unending love. You may be stuck in the bitterness of soul. You may be angry.

But there is a difference between being angry and open to God's healing—and being angry and closed off to God's healing.

Which are you?

The healing process is long. Faith grows back slowly.

Good thing He is way more capable than us. His compassion will always be stronger.

Journal

Day Six:
Oh, But the Heartache

I loathe my life; I will give free utterance to my complaint; I will speak in the bitterness of my soul. I will say to God, Do not condemn me; let me know why you contend against me. Job 10:1-2

I don't think I have to explain the sentiment here. It may mirror some of your own thoughts. Do you hate what life has become? Maybe you question whether it can ever be good again. The rest of your life stretches before you as a big, vast emptiness. All you can see is the redundant pain and lethargy, every day, for the rest of your life.

I don't think Job had any qualms about vocalizing his vexation. Hopefully, you feel the same freedom to speak yours to God. Hopefully, this devotional is showing you it's okay to do so. Expression of the pain, in written form or verbal, is a healthy way of release. Give yourself permission. God's Word does.

Job's honest question above ... why do you contend against me? We ask why so often. *Why this way? Why them? Why me? Why are You testing me, Lord?* Aren't the questions the hardest part? They are excruciating. The unknowns are haunting.

Have you ever felt that if God loved you so much, why has He crushed you so badly? Job said, "Your hands fashioned and made me, and now you have destroyed me altogether." (Verse 8) It doesn't make sense to our broken heart. God is my Creator — and yet, it feels like He wrecked me.

I read Job's diatribe in chapter 10, looking for the golden nugget — that little piece of hope — that small glimmer of eternal perspective to seep through and bring a little light. I read chapter 10 and sought out the smidgen of spiritual understanding to brighten the speech. Something to point out in this devotional entry and offer encouragement.

But I found none. In this particular section of Job's response, I just saw pain. I just saw anguish. I just saw heartache. Venting. Questions. Burden.

So why did I include it? It's kind of depressing. Wouldn't it be *discouraging* to read this when a person is already struggling?

Well, sometimes it actually helps.

There are simply moments when all feels dark. Moments when the intellectual knowledge that life is more than the current pain doesn't change an ounce of your perspective. There are moments when the logical acknowledgment that healing will come doesn't help you feel any better. There are moments when the matter-of-fact admission that God is in control doesn't lessen the chokehold.

There are just moments—days—that just suck.

I wanted you to know, if that's where you are today, it's okay. Job was there. God didn't give up on him. He won't give up on you. Job learned some hard lessons. You may learn some hard lessons. His story wasn't done. Your story isn't done either.

I included this portion of Scripture, this moment in Job's life, to let you know that it's normal. Take one more breath. Feel the life flow in and out. Let the pain wash over you. Let the walls that you are trying so badly to hold together fall apart for a while and just realize:

It's okay to have these seasons. Just remember it's a season.

Journal

Day Seven:
Save Me, O Lord

Save me, O God! For the waters have come up to my neck. I sink in deep mire, where there is no foothold; I have come into deep waters, and the flood sweeps over me. Psalm 69:1-2

If these words seem to identify how you are feeling, we share a bond. And we share a bond with the psalmist. I have often said the pain of my widowhood felt like drowning.

Images come to mind with these verses. Images of thick mud clasping my feet. Images of waves tossing me as I'm powerless to fight against them. Images of coughing and gagging and fighting for breath as the tyrannical swells try to suffocate me.

These images personify the living powers of grief inside me. We wait for "healing." We wait for God to *do* something to make it better. We wait for some kind of deliverance.

The psalmist said, "Deliver me from sinking in the mire; let me be delivered ... from the deep waters. Let not the flood sweep over me, or the deep swallow me up." (Ps. 69:14-15) Does that sound like your desperate plea? For goodness' sake, Lord, don't leave me here! Don't let this grief consume me and swallow me whole!

I find it interesting that of all the ways David could express how he felt, he chose water ... flood ... the deep. There's something inherently terrifying about water when you've lost control ... when you're stuck and the waters are rising to your throat ... when the waves are pounding against you. It naturally hijacks your focus and energy. Fear and survival kick in.

I think about Peter who got out of the boat onto the waves. (Good for him! That's more than any of the others did!) He did try. But those waves! Those crazy, crashing turbulent waves! They got to his psyche. And after Jesus grabbed the sinking Peter, He asked, "Why did you doubt?"

Ummm ... isn't it obvious? The water! The storm! The chaos!

Oh yes, deep waters can make us doubt. Are you doubting? You know who else doubted? John the Baptist. The man about whom Jesus said, "Among those born of women there has arisen no one greater than John the Baptist." Wow. John was the first to recognize the deity of Jesus (in the womb!). His entire calling, his entire anointing was to prepare the way for the Messiah. When he baptized Jesus, he had the supernatural experience of hearing God's voice, physically seeing the anointing of God fall upon Jesus and the heavens splitting open. Holy moly, can you imagine?

Yet ... in Matthew 11 we see him send some of his disciples to Jesus to ask, "Are the One?" Ummm ... what? Didn't he know more than anyone? But you see, John was in prison, time had passed, Jesus wasn't declaring Himself the way some thought He would, nor operating the way most expected of the Messiah. Even John wrestled with doubts. And he needed some reassurance, just like us.

"Answer me, O Lord, for your steadfast love is good; according to your abundant mercy, turn to me ... draw near to my soul, redeem me." (Ps. 69:16 & 18) If we remind ourselves of anything, let it be what the psalmist did. There is never a time when the cares of this life can drown out God's steadfast love. In our grief it is sometimes hard to hear His voice over the waves crashing.

But never have I read a story where God despises the one whose faith is sinking in the mud, trapped in the chaos of tragedy. He knows we are frail.

But God is faithful to us in our humanity. To ransom. To redeem.

Even grief isn't stronger than His love.

Journal

Day Eight:
But, God why?

Today also my complaint is bitter ... Oh, that I knew where I might find him, that I might come even to his seat! I would lay my case before him and fill my mouth with arguments. Job 23:2-4

Job was a little heated, can you tell?

He wished God was like an earthly king, where he could physically go and petition his case—explain why He should intervene, explain why this shouldn't have happened.

After my husband was killed, I would have gladly laid my case before Him for why He should have left my husband here on earth. You've probably had similar thoughts—wishing God was physically accessible to plead before, vent before, or even erupt before.

Or maybe to demand explanations. Job said, "I would know what he would answer me and understand what he would say to me." If God could just explain His reasoning—if He could just tell me why!

Yep, I thought that. Would the logic of an answer make us feel better? Maybe. Maybe not. Does our confusion about God's purpose mean a purpose is not there? Nope.

Pain is simply all-consuming sometimes.

Sorrow can easily consume our logic, even when logic is accessible. But I doubt we could even comprehend God's answer even if He gave us one, since He weaves such a complex web of intricate human interaction throughout past and present and future with our lives and others' lives all in a massive tapestry of human time.

I find it interesting what Job went on to remind himself. "He is unchangeable, and who can turn Him back? What He desires, that He does. For He will complete what He appoints for me." (Job

23:13) Job reminded himself that God has a purpose and a will that we cannot change. He has set out to accomplish certain things, and He will complete them. Sounds so full of faith, right? Or maybe it's resignation. But even with that oh-so-spiritual-sounding reminder, listen to what Job says next. Surprisingly it's not an ode of trust and worship. "I am terrified at His presence; when I consider, I am in dread of Him. God has made my heart faint..." (Job 23:15-16)

Wow! Definitely not the cozy, comfortable kind of faith.

It's easy to trust God when all you hear is 'He wants to bless you,' and 'He wants you to prosper.' But once you have tasted tragedy and come face to face with the fact that sometimes God's plan is painful and He doesn't immunize us from the broken world in which we live, it can be a little unsettling. The innocent bubble has burst. Naivety is gone.

What else does God have in store? we may think.

I used to sing songs that said things like, "refine me" and "have Your way in me." Did I really mean them? Or did I really mean, "Have Your way as long as it doesn't hurt too much or make me too uncomfortable"?

The most poignant verse in this section is verse 10. "But He knows the way that I take; when He has tried me, I shall come out as gold." Job was angry, bitter and confused. He wanted an answer from God! He didn't understand why God allowed what He had. But, he still knew that once God was done, he would be refined like *gold*. I find it so interesting that a subterranean faith was coexisting with all Job's bitterness.

Friend, know that even while you are angry and hurting, you can still be willing to let God work in you. Is your goal to come forth as gold, beautiful and precious, or is your goal for the anger to eat you up from the inside and crumble your spirit?

We don't have to deny our anger or bitterness. But we do have a choice on how we approach God with it ...

Willingly or unwillingly.

Journal

Day Nine:
The Apathy That Comes

So I hated life, because what is done under the sun was grievous to me, for all is vanity and a striving after wind.
Ecclesiastes 2:17

When Solomon wrote these words, he wasn't dealing with grief. But much of what he says in the book of Ecclesiastes illustrates how I felt for a long while after I lost my husband.

Apathetic. Numb. Indifferent. Cold. Detached from life, from hope, from anything resembling feeling spiritual. That apathy made me second-guess everything about myself. If there was a sentence that hung over my head as I processed my grief, it was, *"What is the point of any of this?"* What was the point of life, of all the effort? What was the point of fighting the battle, only to face another one?

In my pain, I didn't just see *my* pain. I now understood the vast amount of hurt residing in the world. My eyes were opened. I was no longer in my ignorant bubble. I recognized how many others sat at home, like me, burdened with their own turmoil, their souls silently screaming. My heart became heavy and grieved for the enormity of it all. All the world appeared as an endless cycle of pain, a black hole of suffering. And it broke my spirit and sucked all my hope dry. Thus, the response is apathy. Feeling nothing as opposed to everything.

Solomon had great wisdom. As he observed the world around him, he got depressed. He saw life as a pointless cycle. "What does man gain by all the toil? ... All things are full of weariness." (Ecc. 1:3 & 8) In grief we often struggle with apathy. The "weariness" of it all. What is the point of the grass being mowed and the floors swept? Our drive and passions have evaporated. Nothing feels the same. Beloved hobbies and even ministry can feel futile and unsatisfying.

Apathy is normal in grief. We feel the void. Just like Solomon, we cry the meaninglessness of it all. The purpose of life feels forgotten—like a mist we can't quite catch. The monotonous, painful redundancy blares like a dull siren in our hearts.

One thing I have always concluded about the odd book of Ecclesiastes is that if there is proof that man cannot be self-fulfilled with the earthly components of life—it's here. In chapter 2, Solomon describes how he had everything a man could desire: money, possessions, accomplishments, women, power, fame and wisdom. And yet ... He looked at life and said it was meaningless. Hollow. Monotonous.

And if we keep our eyes on this human existence, it does feel meaningless. Lord knows, we all understand this earthly existence is painful. There must be something beyond. Grief and trauma can easily strip away proper spiritual perspective. My eternal outlook became clogged and blurred when grief hit. All I could see was the current pain and void. The problem was, that wasn't the only reality surrounding me. There were other truths and realities, but my feelings weren't consumed by *them*. That's why it skewed my perspective.

Maybe grief and tragedy should naturally stimulate our eternal perspective—make us willing to shed fleshly constraints and gain a more spiritual focus. (You know, remind us what's truly important and where our hope truly lies!) But sometimes it can have the *opposite* effect, giving apathy and doubt more fertile ground. This is why grief can be so burdensome to someone struggling with their faith. It can blur the perspective that should bring hope and peace in the storm. Our focus can be sucked down, like Solomon, to the weariness of it all.

If you're feeling numb—numb to your faith, numb to God, numb to life's enjoyments, numb to everything *but the pain*—I want to remind you of something: numb means nerves have been damaged, it does not mean they are beyond repair.

Numb isn't permanent. Numb isn't the finale. Numb is a dictator whose rule will wane. What perspective do you feel God needs to morph today?

Journal

Day Ten:
Lessons from Paul

For we were so utterly burdened beyond our strength that we despaired of life itself. 2 Corinthians 1:8

It is frustrating when people say something like, "God will not place more on you than you can bear." Ever heard that? What does that mean, anyway? Don't they realize you are already living with something more than you can bear? Is that supposed to mean we aren't allowed to crumble because, by golly, if God allowed it, you can bear it? Suck it up, buttercup.

This saying is a casual translation from Paul's writing in 1 Corinthian 10. But Paul later wrote to the same church and said the verse above. *Utterly burdened. Beyond our strength. Despaired of life itself.*

Wait a minute. You mean even strong Christians have those times? Yes!

The word Paul uses for despair in this verse means to be utterly at a loss, renouncing hope. I mean, come on, just tell Paul that God doesn't give him anything more than he can handle. That encourages everyone, right? (I'm being sarcastic, if you can't tell.)

Now, I can't be fair and bring attention to this "hopeless" verse without showing Paul's next statement. "But that was to make us rely not on ourselves but on God who raises the dead ... On Him we have set our hope that He will deliver us again." (2 Cor. 1:9)

Faith is not living in denial of the extreme torment of the storm, of the despair, of the struggle. Faith is totally acknowledging it. And being willing to hold tight anyway.

If you are anything like I was, verse 9 doesn't magically make all the feelings resonating from verse 8 go away. *I mean, come on, Lord, can't You teach me to rely on You in other ways besides taking my loved one?* Let's be real. Those thoughts peck our brains. Why this way? Is it our fault they're dead because we had to learn a lesson?

I can't offer an answer for how or why God works. I ain't that smart. But I can be honest and say that the death of my husband brought about an honest look at the frailties of my faith in a way *nothing* else would have.

If I embrace the honesty to spew my confusion and anger to God, I can know that God is big enough to handle it. *But I must also be big enough to embrace the honesty with myself* and see what has risen to the surface in the refiner's fire. It's not always good.

It is easy to think that super "spiritual" people like Paul aren't brought down by life's circumstances. But there is no such thing as that kind of human. Spiritual people are still affected. Spiritual people still struggle. Spiritual people can be brought down temporarily by the storms of life.

If you already experience the great burden of grief, don't let shame, guilt or embarrassment muddy the waters even more. Let's clear something up: *The emotions you deal with are not equivalent to your faith.* They are not synonymous with it or the summation of it. The caliber of your faith is not defined by the crazy emotions you feel, nor is it defined by their absence.

Emotions are always the first thing to leap into a fight and they are the last thing to reach the summit of peace. Don't let those wavering things be the definition of your faith or your worth. Identify them for what they are. Emotions. Recognize they have to heal.

So be okay with letting them.

Journal

Day Eleven:
When I Can't See

After this Job opened his mouth and cursed the day of his birth. And Job said: "Let the day perish on which I was born ... Let that day be darkness!" Job 3:1-4

I grew up in the church and therefore heard the story of Job. In fact, it was one of my mother's favorites. She always pointed to the fact that Job lost so much, and yet his first response was to fall to the ground and worship. (Job 1:20) I admired that. Then I faced my own tragedy. My first response (pardon me while I clear my throat) was not to worship the Lord. Far from it, actually.

Though the Christian community may preach about his initial response, it took me a while to realize Job had other responses, too. Like venting his bitterness at God and cursing the day of his birth in the verse above.

Romans 8:18 says, "For I consider that the sufferings of this present time are not worth comparing with the glory that is to be revealed." I felt like a bad Christian when those verses didn't comfort me. I felt backwards—upside down. The light at the end of the tunnel didn't feel like enough. I wrestled with trying to reconcile what I believed with how I felt. I struggled with the aftershocks that kept coming and rocking me off balance.

Sometimes when the dust settles and reality sets in, when shock wears off and the restlessness increases, when we are stuck in the leftovers of life ... for a while, we feel worse. And this can make us feel even more hopeless because we question why we aren't getting better. Doubts rekindle. Depression gains more ground. Apathy spreads. *What's wrong with me?*

I can still admire Job's initial reaction. But, boy, I can also relate to his secondary responses. Those *later* reactions and those follow up questions, those ripples of change that reach into unforeseen places, those eruptions that catch us off guard.

Many describe later periods of grief as a different kind of pain from the beginning. As the intensity lessens of the *initial* reactions, it gives rise to the *long-term* reactions. The grief shifts from a raw open wound to an infection spreading its bacteria into the unseen areas of the soul. The denial wears off. The shock wears off. Survival mode wanes. People's initial sympathy morphs into expectations of normalcy. What we're left with is a more vivid reality of what life now is, staring us in the face, and we aren't sure we want to see it. I braced myself for all those "firsts," but those seconds and thirds hurt too because the timeline of my life kept plodding along and the distance pained my heart. Like a drifter floating away from the island where there is safety and hope, and all that drifter can do is watch as the island fades into the distance.

And so, for me, the depression came later. I couldn't see a way out of this new life I didn't want. I couldn't figure out what my goals were. I couldn't figure out how to get better. I couldn't figure out how to make *anything* better. And so, the blackness of despair trickled in and I didn't want to try anymore.

If you are sinking into a depression because you feel you should be better or the hopelessness hasn't waned, or because you don't understand why you struggle more now than you did before, be encouraged. Even this is normal and even this we can look into the Scripture and see.

Job went on in verses 24-26 to say, "My sighing comes instead of my bread, and my groanings are poured out like water. ... I am not at ease, nor am I quiet; I have no rest, but trouble comes." As I read some of the things Job said, they were far from the calm spiritual response he had in chapter 1.

Just like Job, you may go through many phases in processing your struggle. Don't worry. These secondary responses will need to run their course, just as God's compassion will run its course ... all the way to the end of time.

Journal

Day Twelve:
When God Feels Far Away

As a deer pants for flowing streams, so pants my soul for you, O God. My soul thirsts for God. Psalm 42:1-2

If you're like me, you may read these words and think of the well-known praise song, which oozes a message of, "I love you Lord and I want more of you." And (*cough, cough*) that just ain't how we feel right now, right?

Actually, the author of this psalm didn't feel that way either. His imagery relays desperation — thirst — how dry he felt — a.k.a., far from God. The next verse says, "My tears have been my food day and night while they say to me all the day long, 'where is your God?'" (Ps. 42:3)

Not quite the same gist as the praise song. The writer wasn't in a good place. He was broken. Crying. Burdened. Even others were asking where his God was. They could see his torment.

What I find *really* interesting in this psalm is verse 4, where the psalmist describes how he used to lead throngs of people into the house of God with glad shouts and songs of praise. He was a worship leader! But did you catch it?

Used to. Past tense.

He was remembering those good, old, *untainted* days. In a broken place of life, he reminisces about the times when he had been so full of praise. But now? Now he wasn't. He was dry.

After my husband was killed, I would remember all the times I led worship, led Bible studies, and raised my hands in praise. And all of that felt so distant from where I was. None of that was happening anymore. My soul had shriveled. I knew I needed God, but struggled to have any desire to draw near to Him.

That's where the psalmist was. *My soul pants for you.*

Now for the best part of this psalm—verse 5: "Why are you cast down, O my soul, and why are you in turmoil within me? Hope in God; for I shall again praise him, my salvation and my God."

This may sound too hopeful for you, but hold on. Did you notice the clincher? *I shall again ...* That is *future* tense. The praise hadn't happened yet! The writer was *still* in a dark, dry place. He still wasn't oozing with praise and gladness.

Yet. Ah, what a beautiful word.

He was *reminding* himself that the day would come again. Sometimes, in the deep waters, we don't need to deny the fact that we aren't "feeling" it, but we can make a statement—a *statement* of faith. "It will happen again. Maybe not today. But one day."

Even when we don't feel full of faith, that simple statement *is an act of faith.*

The psalmist knew his season would not last. He knew God well enough to know His love would endure longer than the pain.

The psalmist wasn't "there" yet. You may not be, either. You may think you never will be. Maybe you remember the innocent praise you could offer before "it" happened. Maybe you feel dry, like the desperate, dehydrated deer the writer referred to. You, too, are thirsty for God yet can't quite stir up the old desire for Him.

We are not alone in our struggles. We aren't bad Christians for feeling dry. We aren't bad Christians for having a season of struggle and pain and depression.

God is big enough to woo you back.

So be okay with letting Him.

Journal

Day Thirteen:
God's Grace in Our Anger

Now the LORD God appointed a plant and made it come up over Jonah, that it might be a shade over his head, to save him from his discomfort. Jonah 4:6

We often hear about how Jonah ran from God. We hear about the great fish God sent to swallow him to bring him to repentance. We hear how Jonah did eventually go preach to the city of Nineveh. (With a bit of divine coercion, that is.)

But what is really interesting to me is the rest of the story. Jonah sat embittered over the fact that Nineveh repented and that God *accepted* their repentance. "But it displeased Jonah exceedingly, and he was angry." (Jon. 4:1) Umm … if you ever want a straight-to-the-point verse about someone being angry at God — a prophet no less — here it is. In Jonah's case, he was mad that God had *the nerve* to be compassionate toward this foreign nation (Israel's enemy.) It may seem weird to us because we understand God's love to be universal. (Israel didn't quite get that.) But how often do we get mad at how God chooses to operate in our lives?

Then Jonah said, "O Lord, please take my life from me, for it is better for me to die than to live." (Jon. 4:3) Cue the swoon. Dramatic much?

We can mock Jonah, but his frustration was humanly valid. Typically, we don't want do see God's mercy toward our enemies. We may shake our heads at Jonah's reaction, but if we are honest, we often feel the same way about God's will in our lives. I had just as much "righteous" indignation after He took my husband. I probably thought words not too much different than what Jonah spoke here.

But then God responds to Jonah. "Do you do well to be

angry?" (Jon. 4:4) Lord, have mercy … this. What if God broke through the heavens with an audible voice and asked you this question? The very thought makes me quiver just a bit and swallow a big lump in my throat.

In all honesty, I would have probably answered yes. No part of my human understanding could see God's purpose. Wouldn't my husband better serve Him … alive?

Do you have your own arguments?

Now we get to our verse in our heading. God appointed a plant to shade Jonah, to save him from discomfort. Oh, my heart. Jonah was sulking! And even in Jonah's pity party God gave him a piece of comfort. That verse right there makes me marvel. His mercy never ends. Even in our complaining. Even in our distrust. Even in our questions. Even while we are shaking our fists at Him.

There are many things I can point to since the death of my husband that show God's provision and mercy over me, even while I questioned Him. I hope you can, too. He never stopped caring. Anger can easily manipulate our focus like blinders on horses. But if we take them off we can often see God's hand in the background sticking by us as He promised.

Self-pity is a dangerous thing. For thirty-three years of my life I "knew" tragedy happened every day, yet I never really questioned God's goodness, His sovereignty, or His will.

But when tragedy happened to me, I had to rethink it. Ugh! My own hypocrisy stank! I concluded that God was either *still* good, or He never was. It could not be contingent upon my position in life.

Friend, honesty is good. Honesty with God, but also honesty *with yourself*. Let your prayer be for God to open your eyes.

Journal

Day Fourteen:
The Terrible Comfort We Often Receive

Then Job answered and said: "... miserable comforters are you all." Job 16:1-2

Wouldn't you love to be able to say that out loud sometimes to people? "You are a terrible comforter!" Job actually did. Some people mean well, but their "comfort" can make it worse. It is hard for society to grasp that by trying to make us feel better over a thing we shouldn't feel better about, they actually minimize our pain. And minimizing our pain actually makes it feel *maximized*. It's like telling us we don't have to be as upset as we are. It hurts!

In Job's case, his friends kept saying that he must have done something to deserve God's discipline. And, well, we can see Job's response above. Unfortunately, people are often terrible comforters. They try to find an answer where there is none. They try to help us see the "brighter" side. They try to offer opinions on the whys and hows.

Often someone in grief simply needs to feel people's presence, not their words. This is a universal issue since the beginning of time. Unfortunately, it probably won't change.

Job wondered why his friends even felt the need to keep talking. "What provokes you that you answer? I also could speak as you do, if you were in my place; I could join words together against you and shake my head at you." (Job 16:3-4) Aren't Job's words right on? Judgment. We humans are good at it. People will always have their opinion. And ... share them. People will have their thoughts on why it happened, how you've handled it, how you should have handled it, what you are doing wrong and what you are doing right. Job vented his frustration at his friends' opinions. *"If you were in my shoes, I could string a bunch of words together at you, too. I could shake my head and tell you what you need to do.*

It's so easy to judge from the outside looking in.

But that isn't comfort, as we well know. And like most things in life, we don't understand until we understand. We don't *know* until we know.

Job mentioned a similar sentiment in chapter 13. "As for you, you whitewash with lies; worthless physicians are you all." Wow. Worthless physicians. Trying to heal and doing a lousy job. Have you ever used paint to cover up the poor condition of something? It can hide a lot. Job felt his friends were doing that with their words, trying to slap on a coat of paint to cover the festering ooze. He went on to say, "Oh that you would keep silent, and it would be your wisdom!" Ouch!

Unfortunately for Job, his friends didn't follow his advice and keep silent. They went on for *twenty-four more chapters*, trying to prove their point to Job. Poor Job. He lost ten children, all his financial possessions, and now had to sit with three friends who thought they knew it all.

Job is an ancient book of the Bible, several thousand years old. And yet, Job dealt with the same problem we deal with — the poor ability of people to comfort those who are grieving.

Remember they *mean* well. They do. But more often than not they hurt us more. So, like water off a duck's back, don't take anything too personally. People try. People fail. A lot.

My mother used to say for all the failure of Job's friends in their advice, the fact of the matter is, those friends came and sat with Job in his grief for seven days. *Seven. Days.* Sat with him. In silence. In ashes. In mourning. (Then they started speaking and ruined it. Ha!)

In grief we must often bear the pain along with the brunt of people's ignorance and failed attempts. It becomes an all-inclusive part of the weight of grief. Friend, it is *extremely* easy to let the weed of bitterness and resentment have fertile ground in our hearts when grieving. Pluck those suckers out! We don't want that festering in the already foul waters of grief.

Be free of it.

Journal

Day Fifteen:
Ashamed of My Response

Jesus said ... "Simon, son of John, do you love me more than these?" John 21:15

Peter is the best-known disciple. He is also the easiest to relate to. He is the one who spoke up the most. (Usually to stick his foot in his mouth.) The one who stepped out of the boat. (And the one who failed.) He was the one who had the gall to rebuke Jesus—*to His face!* (Cue the gasp) He is also the one who *swooooore* he would *neeeever* betray Jesus.

Then he did. After Peter's adamant boast, can you imagine the gravity of his choice when it hit him? We have all experienced the humility Peter felt, because we have all failed.

After Jesus died, Peter was so discouraged, so disillusioned, so confused, he walked away from what his life had become and reverted back to what his life used to be. He didn't understand what God was doing. He saw his friend and mentor die. He thought it was over. He went back to what he knew: fishing.

When Jesus found Peter after His resurrection, He sat on the shore of the sea and had a conversation something like this: (My extended, behind the scenes version.)

"Simon Peter," Jesus said, "do you love Me ... really love Me, more than your old life?"

Peter squirmed on the rock on which he sat. "Lord, You know I like You."

Jesus gave a sad smile. "I want you to teach My young followers."

They gazed at the fire while the waves crashed on the shore. Peter felt unnerved. He wasn't qualified to teach anyone. The breeze kicked up, spreading the salty spritz of the sea.

Jesus spoke again. "Peter, are you committed to Me? Loving Me to the utmost?"

Peter stopped chewing. "Lord, You know that I am fond of You."
He cleared his throat of the nerves clogging it.

Jesus poked the fire, stirring the embers. "I want you to care for My
followers."

Peter threw the fish bones to the side, his brows furrowed at the
strange conversation. He wasn't worthy of any of Jesus' requests. His
stomach clenched when Jesus turned to him again.

"Peter, do you ... like Me?"

Peter's heart dropped at the casual word Jesus had resorted to. Why
couldn't he dig up his old passion? His old devotion? He sunk his head
low. "Lord, You know that I like You."

Peter couldn't have still been disillusioned by Jesus' death.
He was alive again, sitting next to him. So why was Peter so
distant and detached? Shame and guilt. These partners in crime
can have long-lasting effects even after the original problem has
been dealt with.

When I lost my husband, I was confused. I was struck. I was
in denial that this could be God's plan. And like Peter, my
confusion made me slink back into the shadows and doubt. I was
ashamed for that response. Ashamed for my lack of faith and the
bitterness I saw instead.

And shame is a powerful thing.

Have you ever felt like Peter? When you feel so full of doubt
and disappointments, so full of your own failure and lack of faith,
that if Jesus stood in front of you and asked, "Are you committed
to Me? Do you love Me with a zealous, unyielding love?" would
you squirm? Would you look for words that seemed less
enthusiastic and hardcore because you didn't "feel" it?

Take heart. You aren't the first. You won't be the last. This is
what Peter went through. Was his story over? Nope. Was his
deadened hope made alive again? Yep. Just look at him in Acts!

Sometimes circumstances throw us for a loop. We struggle,
and that's okay. God, in His patient, loving way, comes to us and
sits by the fire, strikes up a conversation and prods us with His
love.

Journal

Day Sixteen:
When Grief Manipulates Us and Brings Guilt

O LORD, rebuke me not in your anger, nor discipline me in your wrath! For your arrows have sunk into me, and your hand has come down on me. Psalm 38:1-2

I grew up a pastor's kid. I started teaching children's church at fourteen. I joined the music team at sixteen. My husband and I were youth pastors, we taught AWANA, eventually pastored a small church. We counseled and discipled. I was churched. I was solid.

Then God took my husband on a foggy highway. I felt unraveled. I found myself flirting with things I never would have before. I contemplated coping in ways I had criticized others for.

Grief, or more like coping with our grief, can make us do funny things. Illogical things. And sometimes, sinful or unhealthy things. For believers, our burden can feel even heavier because we carry guilt for not handling our grief well. For not maintaining integrity. For not keeping the graceful presence in the storm. For not trusting God. For not feeling the *hope* we are supposed to have. Sometimes we feel guilty for our anger toward God. Sometimes we feel guilty for decisions we have made to cope, distract, or numb ourselves that we know do not line up with Scripture.

I don't know what specific sin David was dealing with when he wrote the verse above, but it is clear he felt God's hand upon him. Divine oppression. Not necessarily a bad thing to feel, but it is a heavy thing. It reminds us of His presence. But it's tough to bear.

David went on to say, "My wounds stink and fester because of my foolishness, I am utterly bowed down and prostrate; all the day I go about mourning." (Verses 5-6) Mourning our loss and then mourning our reactions, our mistakes, our lack of trust, our weakness. Mourning all day. Mourning all night. Mentally and physically affected. Eaten from the inside out. Do you ever feel it compounds? It grows and festers. Infection sets in. At times do you ever look at your life and wonder how to get out of this cave grief has put you in?

In my whole life, I felt my weakest during the raw stages of grief. It revealed every weak point of my faith. While people told me how strong I was, I felt completely feeble. Inside, I scoffed at the lunacy of their conclusion.

David knew it was all exposed to God. "O Lord, all my longing is before you; my sighing is not hidden from you. My heart throbs; my strength fails me..." (verses 9-10) We can actually take courage in the fact nothing is hidden from God. None of our feelings are taking Him by surprise. He has seen and heard it *all*.

So maybe we can accept our own weaknesses. Maybe we can accept that it's okay to not be okay.

God's faithfulness isn't contingent on our faithfulness. God's goodness doesn't hinge upon our performance. And He doesn't stop His purposes just because we are human. *We aren't that powerful.*

How could God ever prove His faithfulness if we never experience our own lack? How can we know what it is for Him to carry us if we are never first weak enough to fall?

If you haven't handled your grief like a pro, be encouraged. Most of us haven't. But don't fall prey to the lie that you must be strong. Let Him be strong. Being weak is actually part of being strong. It gives room for God to be who He said He is.

Because I am weak, I appreciate the victory of standing again. Because I have tasted darkness, the light holds new depths. Because I've been carried, I understand anew compassion and mercy.

Being weak, ultimately, gives room to heal.

Journal

Day Seventeen:
Grief Brings a Feeling of Loneliness

My relatives have failed me, my close friends have forgotten me. The guests in my house and my maidservants count me as a stranger; I have become a foreigner in their eyes. Job 19:14-15

So many feel these words Job uttered. Many feel different forms of rejection, letdown, and disappointment from people they care about. Grief has such a way of changing dynamics in relationships.

It's interesting to me that Job says he felt like a stranger to the people in his household. Do you ever feel like the person you were is gone? Do you feel that when your friends and family watch you, they hardly recognize you? Join the club. Often times, we don't even recognize ourselves. Grief does change you. And while you are under the tyranny of grief, processing the loss, you may feel you have become detached from the person you used to be. It is sad that at our lowest point, some have to feel the severance, the distance, or the morphing of close relationships. More massive changes in an already life-changing circumstance.

Grief can make people uncomfortable. Often, we don't fit into a box they understand. They can't always understand the irrational, temperamental, nonsensical behavior that grief brings. And so, they pull away. Maybe they feel their own rejection when we retreat into our pain. Maybe they feel they lost the friend they were accustomed to having. Maybe they worry about doing or saying the wrong thing and so they surrender to the safety of absence.

Whatever it is, so many grievers feel the loss of close relationships after tragedy strikes.

And to be fair (stick with me — with an open mind), *it is a very hard thing to know how to stick by someone who is grieving*. It's hard for us to even understand the volatile and chaotic monster inside ourselves! How can someone on the outside understand it? Grief doesn't always make sense. It's not always logical. It rears its head at the strangest times. It takes the simplest of things and turns them into an avalanche of emotional upheaval.

Grief is a lonely road. Inherently it is a road only you can walk. No one else lost *exactly* the person and relationship and memories and dynamics and pieces of life as you did. Others can walk beside you, but no one can actually carry the burden of your personal feelings, emotional processing, memories, changes and loss. And because it is such a personal journey, it naturally brings with it an inherent isolation. Oh, that word. *Isolation.* Doesn't that sum it up pretty well?

I noticed in my own grief that there were three distinct types of loneliness. First, I was simply lonely for my husband—the one I lost, the one I missed. But I was also just lonely because I was now by myself, facing life, changes, demands, parenting, social situations—alone. But then there's the third type. And that is the grief itself. Carrying that burden down that isolated road. I call it the trifecta of grief. These three types of loneliness are why grief can be excruciating. So if Job's words ring true to your heart, you are not alone. Let's pray that God brings the strength to offer grace during this rough season to those who fail us.

You can also pray that the changes grief brings can also be good changes. If you don't recognize yourself, or others don't recognize you, maybe it can be for some positive reasons. Growth, maturity, wisdom, compassion … are all things that can grow from loss. Becoming more bold, stepping out of your normal routine (often because you are forced), casting away old inhibitions, your broken heart bonding to a new ministry, can all be byproducts of being thrust upon this unseen path in life.

What might God grow inside you? How might He change you for the better?

Journal

Day Eighteen:
The Lord is My Shepherd

Even though I walk through the valley of the shadow of death, I will fear no evil, for you are with me; your rod and your staff, they comfort me. Psalm 23:4

I know this devotional digs into the darker Scriptures and avoids those "fluffy" ones. But after delving into the darkness and showing you the normality of our struggles, I want to show you now the normality of stepping back into the light. The normality of healing. The normality of thriving again.

There are no famous verses better known for the poetic and peaceful vibes than Psalm 23. *Shepherd. Green pastures. Still waters. Paths of righteousness.* Oh, it's all just so rainbows and butterflies, right?

But dig past that initial vibe. "He restores my soul." Well, how does He restore something if it hasn't first been broken? "You prepare a table before me in the presence of my enemies." Oh, you mean He doesn't take away the hostile environment? Well, bummer.

In verse 4, I want to point out the words, "even though." *Even though* I walk through the valley. *Even though* I'm in the darkness. *Even though* I can't see anything right now but death. *Even though* I'm miserable. *Even though* my faith is in shambles.

Even though are some pretty powerful words.

I *will not fear because you are with me.* Notice it didn't say "when you keep me from deep darkness" or "after you have brought me through deep darkness" that I will fear no evil. This is specifically a reminder that *during* the darkness He is still your shepherd, still with you, still guiding. Like the shepherd that left the ninety-nine to go after the one — the *one* that wandered off, the *one* that got lost, the *one* that was alone, the *one* that ended up deep in the hills. He's *that* shepherd.

The words "valley of the shadow of death" always seemed like bulky phraseology to me. It's more understandable to me (and closer to the original Hebrew) to say, "Even though I walk through the valley of deep darkness." Oh, yes. That picture resonates with me. Cliffs on each side that block the sun. Walls so high there isn't a way to climb them. There is no way out, except *through.*

Just like grief and pain.

God is moved with compassion as we cry. He is crying with us as we mourn. Just as I can't comprehend how God can intimately know seven billion people at the same time and how He can be orchestrating all of human history and future at every given moment; I also can't understand how He can bear with each of us our grief, our sadness, our joys, our disappointments, our pains. Each of us. All the time. How massive His shoulders. How perfect His ability — to feel with all of us at the same time.

Psalm 23 isn't blue skies and butterflies. It's actually a reminder that through the toughest times in life, God leads us, guides us, corrects us, and comforts us. It's a reminder of His ever-present character. And David, of all people, needed to remind himself of that. Remember how much he went through?

And I'm pretty sure we need that reminder, too.

The Lord is my shepherd.

Journal

Day Nineteen:
When There's No Rescue

But when I hoped for good, evil came, and when I waited for
light, darkness came. Job 30:26

It's faith-inducing when we read how God rescued Daniel
from the lions, rescued David from the power of the giant, rescued
Paul from prison and the three Jews from the fiery furnace.

The problem is, when we are not "rescued" from what is
troubling us, we can become disillusioned and our faith wavers.
When we are not rescued, or if we don't feel the divine comfort or
intervention of God, we can start doubting: doubting God, or
doubting ourselves. Maybe we aren't special enough. Maybe we
don't have enough faith. Maybe God doesn't care. Maybe He isn't
as good as everyone says.

In 2 Kings, we are introduced to King Azariah. "He did what
was right in the eyes of the Lord, according to all that his father
Amaziah had done." Ah, so he was a good king. A righteous one.
Fantastic. One who did right in God's eyes. Great! Oh, but look at
verse 5. "And the Lord touched the king, so that he was a leper to
the day of his death." Yikes.

We don't know much else about Azariah. But we know God
didn't rescue him.

In Acts 12, Peter is imprisoned. The church prayed earnestly
for him. God sent an angel, who appeared in the cell, loosened the
chains that bound him, and got him past the guards miraculously.
A.K.A. — rescued him. Yay! Right? But often we skip over the fact
that, five verses before, in Acts 12:2, James, another of the twelve
disciples, had been killed by the sword. God hadn't rescued him.
Or Stephen, in chapter 7 of Acts, who was stoned to death.

I cannot answer for God's whys, whens, hows and whos. But
I can for sure look at all of Scripture and know that God doesn't

rescue everyone, all the time. He never promised to. Sometimes, He allows the horrible. It would have been wonderful to have walked away from our car accident with a living husband and be able to hear the doctors say something like, "We don't know how he survived!" and me being able to respond with, "I know how! It was God."

But that didn't happen. I walked away from the accident without God intervening with a miracle. You're reading this book because God didn't change your awful situation either. And so, we are part of a club we didn't want to belong to: The Grievers. The Hurting. The Broken. A.K.A. — the humans.

Job's words above were followed by this question in Job 31:3. "Is not calamity for the unrighteous and disaster for the workers of iniquity?" It's such a normal question. One most of us think at least once in our lives. For others, it's something we wrestle with for a good while. But the book of Job, if we were to read it in full, is Job's friends basically saying, "You must have done something for God to punish you like this," and Job responding, "I haven't done any evil for God to punish me like this," and God finally stepping in after their constant bickering saying, "Here's the deal … I am God, and you are not."

Job's story, and the examples I gave above, all point to an answer to the question. Is not calamity for the unrighteous? No, not necessarily. It's really for all of us.

Oh, my friend, if you're mad, as I've said in this book before … it's okay. He can handle it. And no one can strip that from you until you're ready. But you are reading this book because you don't want to stay there, right? You, like I was, are trying to reconcile this hard truth — trying to make peace with the fact that it happened and God allowed it. There wasn't a rescue.

Let our prayer be for our minds to echo Job in chapter 1. "The Lord gives, and the Lord takes away. Blessed be the name of the Lord." And mimic Job's attitude, "In all this Job did not sin or charge God with wrong."

Journal

Day Twenty:
The Battle that Comes

How long, O LORD? Will you forget me forever? How long will you hide your face from me? How long must I take counsel in my soul and have sorrow in my heart all the day? Psalm 13:1-2

Can you hear the angst in the psalmist's words? Maybe you have uttered similar words. How long will this pain last? How long, Lord, before You heal me and bring me through it?

If you are anything like me, you had a preconceived notion that grief would have a timetable—that grief was a linear path and would have an end. In reality, grief simply becomes part of you. It seeps into the fabric of who you are instead of staying a heavy cloak thrust upon your shoulders. There is a gradual lessening of grief's chokehold.

David went on to ask, "How long shall my enemy be exalted over me?" He had real-life enemies. But ask yourself today, what is your enemy that is trying to prevail over you? Is it depression? Is it hopelessness? Is it anger? Something else?

One thing is for certain in grief: we are thrust into a spiritual battle—a mighty spiritual warfare. Who will win? *What* will win? Will Satan use it to destroy our faith? Will we become stuck and ineffective? Will bitterness suck the purpose and joy out of us? The pain of grief and tragedy can have a way of tunneling our vision to nothing else but the darkness.

I sure don't want my enemy to triumph over me. I need the light. I need God to open my eyes. Hopefully, you have the same desire even if you don't know how to get there.

David went on in verses 5 and 6, "But I have trusted in your steadfast love; my heart shall rejoice in your salvation." *Rejoice.* Are you cringing at the word? That's okay! Me too! Rejoice doesn't mean feeling giddy and wanting to dance around oozing butterflies and rainbows. It can simply mean standing on the truth and the hope represented by that truth, rather than the darkness you are now in. Remember Psalm 42? "I shall praise you again."

I can acknowledge I am in a pit and also at the same time acknowledge I will not live forever in that pit. And accepting *that* truth *is hope*.

Hope can be a painful thing. We can feel like we are betraying our loved one by feeling hope or happiness. We may even feel we are just setting ourselves up for another terrible disappointment. But Proverbs tells us that, "Hope deferred makes the heart sick." (Pr. 13:12)

Our souls thrive on hope. And our souls become ash without it.

Hope ... is life-giving.

Having hope doesn't mean you will forget your loved one. It doesn't mean you forget your pain. That was hard for me to grasp. Because walking around in sadness felt like the way I proved how much I loved my husband and showed my desire for him to still be here with me.

But when you get to the end of your life, you will not look back and wish you had grieved more, or been depressed more, or sulked in sadness more.

When you get to the end of your life, you will wish you had *lived* more.

And true *life* ... springs from hope.

Journal

Day Twenty-One:
Being "Strong"

I will boast ... of my weakness, so that the power of Christ may rest upon me ... I am content with weaknesses ... For when I am weak, then I am strong. 2 Corinthians 12:9-10

We hear so much about being strong. If you have been thrown into tragedy, most likely at some point someone has told you how strong you are, or encouraged you to "stay strong." Hogwash! After I lost my husband, I began to hate that word. It became tiresome. I didn't want to be strong. I wanted permission to be weak. What does it even mean—to be strong? What do people even mean when they say it? The fact that we have faced the sunlight of another day? (Well, that is strong if the gravity pull of giving up is real.) But it also brings up the question of what we define as weak. What makes us feel "weak"? Is it struggling? Having doubts?

We tend to be embarrassed or ashamed of weakness. Yet that didn't seem to be the attitude of Paul. He actually boasted about it. Imagine an amputee, walking into a room, pointing to his stub and saying, "Look! Look at my disability! It's great, right?" We don't tend to think like that. In fact, we tend to try to hide it.

If there was any moment in time that I felt my weakest, it was during my grief. It highlighted every flaw like a spotlight on a stage. The light shone, revealing all my imperfections. My fears I had always kept well hidden. The cowardice I always diverted attention from. The moral compromise I didn't realize lurked under the surface. The frailty and fragility of my faith came and cracked the well-polished surface. All my weaknesses came like an army storming a fortress. And instead of the strong, mature Christian I always thought myself to be, I saw myself for what I was. Weak.

93

Trauma, grief, heartache.... It peels back all the layers of assumptions and compensations we have formed in life and forces us to look at the bare root of what we are — exposed to the elements. And yet, we can be molded into a person better than before. Grief has the unique power to reveal all our weaknesses, and thus, the power to transform.

Embrace being weak, so you can fall into the arms of the One who carries you on His shoulders, under His wings and in His hands. We often feel that when our faith is weak, we are in a bad position.

But what if we are in the perfect position?

It is literally only then that God's grace can show His sufficiency. The word *weakness* means "lack of strength or capacity. Infirmity. Frailty." Shoot, I'll be the first one to admit I'm weak. I definitely don't have the capacity to shoulder all this pain and confusion and keep myself poised, elegant and cheerful all the time. I'm a mess! And I'll admit it! It is okay to not be okay. It is okay to not have it all together.

When God said, "My power is made perfect in weakness," that word *perfect* means "to perform." When we are weak, God's power is able to perform. There's a principle here. When my kids were little, I cut their food for them, I helped them dress, I buckled them into their car seats. But they got to an age where they would shove my hands away and say, "I can do it, Mommy!" And guess what, I pulled my hands away. I wasn't going to fight them. It's only when we can't do it that God is able to perform. That's why Paul was content in his weakness. Because if he was strong enough to do it himself, he wouldn't have relied on God. He wouldn't have gotten to know, so intimately, the sustainability of Christ.

So maybe we can let ourselves crumble and not feel like a failure. Maybe we *rest* in our weakness.

Journal

Day Twenty-Two:
Why Me ... and Not Them?

Why do the wicked live, reach old age ...? Their offspring are established in their presence ... Their houses are safe from fear, and no rod of God is upon them. Job 21:7-9

Job lost *all ten* of his children. Imagine his anguish. Imagine as he looked at the world around him and saw others, living their lives, living with *their children*. Living without the painful experience he was having to endure. Can you hear the angst and bitterness in Job's words? Can you recognize them in yourself? Can you hear the question in his words — "Why me and not them?" Especially when "them" are people who show no apparent desire to honor God.

It is so easy for bitterness to spring up. Job was very conscious of the fact that many unrighteous people still had *their kids.* Yet he had spent so much effort trying to serve God — to be loyal and pure. God Himself called Job righteous. Yet Job was the one who lost so much.

When I saw people with their husbands, my heart grumbled. *Lucky you.* If you lost your child, seeing others with their children might make you feel that pang of envy. *Lucky you.*

What about people who don't appreciate it? People who don't "deserve" it, even? It defies our sense of justice. Shouldn't good people receive good things and rebellious people receive evil things? The dangers of comparing — it's a slippery slope.

I remember being at the gym, cooling off after a workout, scrolling through my Facebook, when a post made me stop. A friend was praising God that her husband had made it home safe and sound after almost being hit by a semi-truck. I distinctly remember feeling the ugly weed of jealousy in my heart. I wasn't praising God with her. (Horrible, right?) I was mad that her story wasn't my story. My husband didn't come home safe after a meeting with a semi-truck. *Lucky you.*

The problem with comparing is it is often lopsided. We humans have a sickness called "negativity." I wasn't focusing on the fact that God had brought my daughter through the accident, or that He provided money for the funeral, or that He provided a burial plot free of charge, or that He took care of the massive business debt I was left with.

I was only focused on what He took from me.

You see, someone else could have compared their story to my story and grumbled with jealousy because they didn't see God work the same kind of provisions. Or someone else could look at another person's story and grumble because they didn't have the same kind of friends to support them. And on and on it can go.

We often say, "Why me?" But I once heard a pastor say, "Why not you?" Is tragedy reserved for everyone but us? Are we supposed to be exempt? Is heartbreak reserved only for those who "deserve" it, and if so, who decides the definition of that? Are we, as God's people, secretly living with the expectation that our faith in Him should exclude us from the deepest suffering?

Oh, it is a hard topic. Most often we answer with a quick, "Of course not!" but follow it with a just as quick, "But..."

We live in a world of tragedy. We just do. A world of sin and fallen nature and an earth and heavens under its curse. We can't make sense of it. We can't find explanations. There is no riddle to make it logical. It just ... is.

"Should we accept good from God and not accept evil?" Job said to his wife after his life fell apart. And yet he, too, fought this fight against the weed of bitterness, the weed of comparisons. This fight is part of our human condition. We need not feel ashamed of it. But we also need not make a home for it. It will destroy us far worse than the grief itself.

Journal

Day Twenty-Three:
Are There Better Grieving Styles?

And David said to his servants, "Is the child dead?" They said, "He is dead." Then David arose from the earth and washed and anointed himself and changed his clothes. And he went into the house of the LORD and worshiped. 2 Samuel 12:19-20

David had beseeched the Lord, fasting and praying, for seven days, for the life of his sick child. It was so intense, so ardent, that people around David were scared for him. When the child died, his servants were afraid to tell David for fear he would do himself harm. David's response was nothing like his servants expected. They expected him to sink lower. Instead, David arose, washed, dressed and ate. David said, "While the child was still alive, I fasted and wept ... But now he is dead. Why should I fast? Can I bring him back again?" (Verses 22-23)

Not everyone can reach acceptance as quickly as David did that moment. David was able to pick himself up and know that what happened couldn't be changed. It was done. My mother was kind of like that. When she lost her two-year-old daughter to cancer, she started packing her things soon after. In her mind, she had processed the coming death. In her mind, she couldn't change it, so life continued. Taking the sight of her things away helped to move forward.

Some process grief that way. Others are wholly opposite. Often, we compare ourselves with others and compare grieving styles. Then we as humans tend to apply labels to certain behaviors as "stronger" or "better" or "more spiritual" than others. It's a hard topic, but I am going to try to tackle some principles here on what constitutes unhealthy grieving.

Denial. Living in denial prevents you from processing the grief at all. It won't accept the truth of the loss, avoids the reality of the loss, and therefore bars any true healing from coming. The wound festers in secret. **Self-Harm.** Not just physical harm, but torturing yourself with guilt and questions that you cannot change or answer, making reckless decisions that leave you with a string of consequences to bear the weight of in addition to grief. **Bitterness.** When you *refuse* to allow any hope, light or healing to touch you, refuse to laugh again, refuse to join others... it locks you in a prison.

Beyond these principles of unhealthy grieving, we cannot put blanket terms on grieving styles, grieving timetables, or coping mechanisms without boxing in a very abstract and liquid concept of the human soul and minimizing the very personal nature of grief itself.

Acceptance can be a confusing term. We think of someone being *okay* with what happened, and often our hearts revolt against the idea. But maybe acceptance is simply being *honest* about what happened—about the event, the confusion, the feelings and the need to heal.

Maybe part of the acceptance is accepting the fact that no two days will be alike. Acceptance is acceptance of the pain. Acceptance of the anger. Acceptance of the missing. *And even acceptance of the sparks of hope and times of peace. Sometimes even accepting the "good" possibilities of this unrequested, unwanted life.* You accept it as part of you. Accept that it'll change you. Accept that it will have moments of bubbling up inside of you. (Or maybe bursting.) The experience has seeped roots into every part of your being, bringing a new depth of character and strength and compassion.

Don't fall prey to the cycles of comparisons. It's simply you and God. It's God and you. Let God guide your journey, not others, not society, not friends. But Him and His wisdom.

Ask yourself these questions: Am I being *honest* with myself and God? Am I *reaching* for hope? Am I *doing* something to keep my soul active to get outside of my own pain?

Don't fight your grieving process. Accept it. Own it. Work it. But more than anything ... entrust God with it.

Journal

Day Twenty-Four:
The Prayer of the Afflicted

Hear my prayer, O LORD; let my cry come to you ... My heart is struck down like grass and has withered; I forget to eat my bread. Because of my loud groaning my bones cling to my flesh.
Psalm 102:1, 4-5

There is an introduction to this psalm in my Bible. "A Prayer of one afflicted, when he is faint and pours out his complaint before the Lord." Sounds relatable.

This psalm starts with the honest cry of the heartbroken. Hear me, God. Do something. Help me feel not so far away from You. Then it talks about the days passing like smoke in verse 3. That speaks to me. Day after day, the void of life slips by. Somehow a month has passed, six months, a year, three years. Like smoke vanishing, there go my days, slipping from one into the next in this autopilot mode. We can't believe the world keeps turning. How is our life moving on without them?

Then, after eleven verses of pouring out the complaint, the psalmist switches gears in verse 12. "But you O Lord, are enthroned forever; you are remembered throughout all generations." The writers of the psalms put me to shame. They always seem to find a way to worship in their pain, to remind themselves of God's magnificence in spite of it.

So it begs the question—is worship really synonymous with gooey gladness, dancing in celebration or feel-good feelings? Hmmm ... Maybe not. We tend to lump praise and worship together, but they're actually two distinct things.

My only conclusion is they didn't link God's worthiness to the circumstances of this sinful life. I think they expected the heartache much more than we do today. Worship is simply putting God in His proper position. Emotions actually have little to do with it. This is why you can worship even while you are struggling. Even while you are angry and confused. Even when the *praise* hasn't come yet.

Then the writer switches gears again in verse 13. "You will arise and have pity on Zion ... the appointed time has come. For your servants hold her stones dear and have pity on her dust ... For the Lord builds up Zion." It seems odd at first that a "prayer of the afflicted" psalm includes a portion about building up a city. What does that have to do with *anything* when we are struggling? But to an Israelite, the building up of Zion represented the ultimate hope. Zion was the seat of power in God's holy city, representing the rule of David. It represented Israel's righteousness, freedom, and *peace* as a nation. And the city of Zion was in ruins.

This prayer includes this portion as a beacon of hope. It's a reminder that when all feels lost, broken, and shattered in ruins, God will build it again.

In the ruins of our life after grief, we often have to reinvent ourselves, find our new self, and forge a new identity. Let this portion about God rebuilding Zion remind you—even after destruction, God can rebuild. Brick by brick. Stone by stone. Heartstring by heartstring.

So you can read this almost as saying, *"But you will have pity on my life, which has been broken and lies in ruins, and when the appointed time has come, you will rebuild it, for what remains is but stones and dust. And you will rebuild my life."*

Unfortunately, the life you had can never be exactly as it was again. That's what makes grief so hard. The journey requires prying our hands, finger by finger, off what was, to be able to embrace a new future. A new city. A new Zion.

Maybe we can learn from this psalmist. Complete freedom to utter our complaint. And yet, at the same time, remind ourselves of God's position, rebuilding power and attentiveness to our prayers.

Journal

Day Twenty-Five:
Where Else Do I Have To Turn?

When my soul was embittered ... I was brutish and ignorant; I was like a beast toward you. Nevertheless, I am continually with you; you hold my right hand. You guide me with your counsel. Psalm 73:21-24

So, I'm not the only one who responded in a not-so-great manner to God? Whew. You aren't either. Often, we cringe because we just *know* we are the only ones who struggle so much. I don't want to say, "It's okay," because it really isn't okay to respond like a brute toward God. But I will say God is big enough to handle it. That's a safe bet.

Sometimes we aren't honest enough with ourselves to recognize our response for what it is. (That brute beast thing—reacting in the basest of instincts.) It's hard to admit the bitterness inside. I love the second part of what the writer, Asaph, says above. He recognized that even when we are behaving badly, God still has us by the hand. We don't stop being His children. The part I love the most is the reminder that God guides us with His counsel. His Word is always there, unchanging, eternal, a strong tower, and our anchor. Even when we feel detached from it.

It is an amazing thing to know the character of God. When I retreated from my faith, I knew God enough to know He would woo me back. I rested in that fact when I could rest in nothing else. But it begged the question in my mind: Why would He go through the effort? Why come after me when I disconnected from Him? Distanced myself? When I pushed Him away? When I shook my fist? Doubted? Why would I be worth the effort to woo back?

Oh, but for the love of God.

In verse 25, Asaph says, "Whom have I in heaven but you?" This is the meat of this whole section. When I peel away all the emotions, all the grievances, all the chaos—when I get to the core of my heart—who else is there, really, for me to turn to? Where else do I go? Who else can I turn to for hope beyond the here and now and hope beyond this broken world?

If you need a reminder today that we as humans will fail, here it is. "My flesh and my heart may fail, but God is the strength of my heart." (verse 26) We will mess up. We will be overwhelmed. We will be weak and frail. And so, we depend on a God who doesn't fail, who doesn't get tired, who doesn't give up. That's the God I know. Yes, He allows the pain. Yes, He allows evil for a time. But He's always in the background, working.

"When I tried to understand all this, it was oppressive to me ... till I entered the sanctuary of God." (verse 16) Stop and reread those words. Asaph wasn't talking about grief, but doesn't it fit? When we try to apply human reasoning to understand the whys and hows, it's all so oppressive. It. Just. Hurts. And if that's where our focus stays, it continues being oppressive. But when we enter the sanctuary of God ... when we allow His presence to penetrate ... when we allow a surrender ... then peace can filter in.

The idea of spending time in His presence may feel like forcing a round peg into a square hole. The desire may not be there. But that's okay. *Feelings don't define your faith.* Remember? Do you think David felt all gooey inside when he flooded his bed with tears? Or was Job feeling all bubbly when he cursed the day of his birth? Or did Joseph feel warm and cozy when he sat in a dark prison cell year after year for simply doing the right thing?

I don't think so. You can hardly find any hero of the Bible that you cannot point to an extreme low point in their life. A time where they fell into depression, weakness, poor choices, questioning, grief, anger, doubts, etc. We are in good company.

Root yourself in the truth of God's faithfulness. *Rest* in the knowledge of His character. And, when you're ready, reach for His presence.

Journal

Day Twenty-Six:
The Small Steps

She had heard the reports about Jesus and came up behind him in the crowd and touched his garment. For she said, "If I touch even his garments, I will be made well." Mark 5:27-28

This woman suffered for years. We are told for twelve years she had dealt with a discharge of blood, a medical condition no one could solve. For twelve years she had been frail and sickly. For twelve years she had been considered unclean by society and most likely considered an outcast. For twelve years she spent all she had on physicians. After all that, she was left with no answers, destitute, hopeless and worse off.

Then she heard about Jesus.

You know why I love this woman? Because I relate to her. She wasn't like the centurion who had a commanding, unwavering faith. She wasn't like Peter who had the guts to step out of the boat to try something crazy like stepping onto liquid. She wasn't like the four men who lowered their paralytic friend through a roof to capture Jesus' attention and healing in a bold, tenacious way.

This woman was nothing like that. By all accounts, she would be considered timid and fearful, hesitant and cautious. This woman didn't have the courage to meet Jesus face to face. Even as desperate as she was, she didn't have the strength to expose herself to seek His attention. She couldn't bring herself to grab His hand or even call out to Him. She didn't step into His path and beg for His compassion with her story like so many others had during Jesus' ministry.

She stayed in the shadows. She didn't speak a word. She only had the courage to risk the basest of actions. Her courage was only strong enough to stay *behind* Him where He "couldn't see" and where she thought she could stay invisible. All she had strength to do was touch a piece of fabric that trailed behind Him. To touch His hem. To grip the *very edge* of His presence.

I relate to this woman. Because sometimes that's where we humans are. Our strength has shriveled. Our boldness has evaporated. We are desperate and dry. We need healing but don't have the fortitude to take hold of Jesus and cry out, "Heal me!" We feel broken and destitute and frail. So, we stay in the shadows. And we struggle to risk the smallest of measures—struggle to expose ourselves—struggle to reach out in such meager ways because it seems so pointless.

What is even more beautiful in this story is Jesus' response. He stops. Think about that. He *stops*. In all of the crowd and chaos, He stops to give attention to this seemingly less-than-courageous woman. No rebuke. No chastisement. Among a throng of people pressing for His attention, He stops and acknowledges her timid action. Now the woman is terrified. In her quest to remain hidden, He calls her out. In her fear of being exposed, He puts her in the spotlight. But He stops to *honor* her—honor her weakened faith— her risk—and honor her choice. That choice to take that small step.

Because that small step was a big step. That weakened faith was a strong faith. That timidity was courageous. Sometimes we forget that. When we don't measure up to the tenacity of others or don't have the strength to be bold and hopeful like others or how we ourselves *used* to be, we lose sight of the fact that God acknowledges the smallest of steps.

Even beyond acknowledging her, Jesus *healed* her.

When we are weak and we can only reach for the very edge of His being, it still means something. Whether you feel strong enough or energetic enough or worthy enough to reach out to Him, focus on Jesus' response to this woman. He stopped. He turned. Notice how rewarded the woman's most basic action was. Jesus called it faith. Jesus called her daughter. Jesus showed pleasure. If you don't have the strength for grand gestures or bold faith, be encouraged. You have a God who acknowledges the small steps. In fact, He honors them.

Journal

Alisha Bozarth

Day Twenty-Seven:
Mercy for the Crippled

And David said to him [Mephibosheth], "Do not fear, for I will show you kindness for the sake of your father Jonathan, and I will restore to you all the land of Saul your father, and you shall eat at my table always." 2 Samuel 9:7

Mephibosheth was born grandson to King Saul. Heir to the kingdom of Israel. But as an adult he lived the poor life of a cripple. As a young boy, not only did Mephibosheth lose that royal inheritance, lose his father and grandfather, but he also lost the simple ability to walk. His nurse dropped him and crippled his feet as she fled when news came of Israel's defeat in battle. Instead of growing up as royalty, he grew up disabled in a place called Lo-Debar, which was a barren, desolate land.

Mephibosheth's life can resemble our grief-stricken lives. The things that have fallen apart. The things that have been stripped away by force. The things that can never be recovered. It can feel as if grief stole all the good things away. Grief can make you feel like you are living in that desolate wasteland called "*Your Life Now.*"

Mephibosheth would never be in line to the throne. He would never again be able to walk. His dead father couldn't be returned. His life had become nothing but living in dread of the new king finding him and killing him to prevent competition for the throne.

The story of Mephibosheth is a beautiful one of grace, kindness, and restoration. The new king, David, *did* find him in his barren life. And the king *invited him to his table*. It was an invitation to a new life. An invitation to step away from the shame and fear that had followed him since he was a boy. An invitation to step out of the shadows and back into the light.

But Mephibosheth had a choice.

He could have remained bitter at King David. After all, it was David who took the kingdom from his family. (By God's sovereign design, of course.) His pride could have risen up and refused the king's compassion. In his bitterness, he could have spat in the face of David's offer and brought a swift end to his miserable life. Or he could accept the invitation.

Grief takes us into the shadows. Dark things live there. But the redeeming grace of the King still calls you to join Him at the table.

There is such a thing as putting yourself in a position for healing.

And such a thing as not.

You cannot close yourself off from God and then complain when He isn't healing you. Join Him at the table. I'm sure Mephibosheth didn't feel comfortable at first. There were probably crazy emotions resurfacing as he was taken under the wing of the very man whose calling changed the course of his life and his family.

Don't feel like a hypocrite if you go to church or read your Bible and feel no attachment or emotional response—or maybe even feel anger. You aren't a hypocrite to keep going. *You are putting yourself in position.* As adults, we often don't *feel* like going to work, but we go and cycle through the motions. We don't often *feel* the butterflies of love in the presence of a screaming child throwing a tantrum, but we take care of the child anyway. Maturity is doing the work, even when emotions are lacking. Emotions will often have to catch up.

And so, when our faith has been damaged, we come to the King's table—with our hurts, our betrayals, our bitterness, our confusion—and learn who He is once again. We learn to trust again. We learn His character once again.

And we put ourselves in a position of healing.

Journal

Day Twenty-Eight:
The Unexpected Healing

There were many lepers in Israel in the time of the prophet Elisha, and none of them was cleansed, but only Naaman the Syrian. Luke 4:27

Jesus was speaking here about Naaman from the story in 2 Kings chapter 5. The story of Naaman, the leper, is an interesting one. But I find Jesus' point even more interesting: there were other lepers during the time of Elisha. Yet we don't hear about them pursuing healing. We don't read their story of restoration. Israelites, God's people, weren't seeking God's healing. It was a Gentile.

There is such a thing as not reaching for healing. There is such a thing as sinking your feet into your misery. There is such a thing as accepting the bitter condition you are in and not seeking God's restoration.

When we look at Naaman's story (read it in 2 Kings 5), his healing happened nothing like he thought. He almost didn't obey the ridiculous instructions the prophet gave him. Wash in the dirty Jordan River? There were plenty of nice rivers in his homeland. Why did he have to travel all this way just to dip his body in a river? The prophet didn't even come out, for goodness' sake, and perform any pomp or ceremony or rituals. Why *did* he travel all that way? Naaman threw a fit.

Preconceived ideas can hinder a lot of things. Expectations of God, expectations of yourself, and expectations of others can manipulate your views. These unspoken, sometimes unconscious expectations, along with timetables, comparisons and self-pity can do exactly what it did to Naaman—make you want to walk away and say forget it.

But notice what Naaman's servant said. "My father, it is a

great word the prophet has spoken to you; will you not do it?" (2 Kings 5:13) His servant had a point. While Naaman focused on the silliness of the command, his servant focused on the fact that the prophet had promised healing. One statement. Two men. Two different focuses. The servant basically asked, "What do you have to lose?" He had come all that way, so why not try it and obey?

And so, I'd ask you that. *What do you have to lose?* What do you have to lose by slowly, deliberately, and painfully grasping hope? What do you have to lose by opening up the bud of your heart to what God may be leading you toward? What do you have to lose by allowing the pain to be channeled into something healthy and allowing God to take the brokenness and create new purpose? I'll answer for you. You have nothing to lose. But you do have something to gain.

Grief smacks us before a crossroad. Actually, it smacks us before a three-branched crossroad. One takes you down a path where bitterness and apathy drown your faith and joy. The second takes you down a path where your faith remains but is detached, cold, and has no preeminence in your life. The third path is clutching your faith, even when you don't think it's accomplishing anything, and giving it time to grow fresh and deeper roots.

Sometimes that crossroad is before us daily. Sometimes hourly. Two paths lead to the dry spiritual desert. One leads to restoration.

I don't want to be one of the people who are absent of a story of restoration. I don't want to be like one of the lepers in the house of Israel who never reached for healing. What about you? I want to be like Naaman, who although it came in an unexpected way, although he threw fits of rage, and although he almost walked away, decided there was nothing to lose in reaching for it.

Even if it means crawling that path with scraped knees, bloody hands, and a heavy heart, isn't the healing worth it?

Journal

Day Twenty-Nine:
Help My Unbelief

Immediately the father of the child cried out and said, "I believe; help my unbelief!" Mark 9:24

A father. A demon-possessed son. And Jesus. A triangle of desperation and expectation.

This man had lived for years with his son being convulsed and taunted by an evil spirit. For years, he lived as an outcast. For years he watched his son being tormented while he could do nothing. Don't you know those years wore him down?

Then he went to the disciples, whom he heard were casting out demons and healing. Hope stirred inside him, I'm sure. But the disciples couldn't heal his son. That father walked away with hopes dashed. I can only imagine what he was feeling that moment.

Have you ever been in a situation where hope was painful? It was too disappointing. Too scary. Too dangerous. By the time this father came to Jesus, I wonder if he was afraid to hope. He said to Jesus in verse 22, "But if you can do anything, have compassion on us." The words "if you can" caught Jesus' attention. If Jesus had a sarcastic side, I can hear it as He repeats those words in verse 23. *If I can?*

But I love the honesty that spilled from this overwhelmed and disheartened father when Jesus said anything is possible for one who believes: "I believe; help my unbelief." At first glance it feels so contradictory to say such a thing. But at a deeper glance, especially within our own hearts, it's not contradiction. It's honesty. It's relatable. It's the dirty truth.

Because we live in a mortal frame where faith and unbelief play tug-of-war inside us. And, when tragedy, grief, or other events that leech the life-giving nutrients from our souls come along, the unbelief starts winning the competition.

Can faith and unbelief coexist? Yes. This father simply admitted it.

Look at Martha in John chapter 11. Her brother Lazarus died. Jesus came. This was the basics of their conversation:

"If you had been here, my brother would not have died," Martha said.

"Your brother will rise again."

"Yes, I know, in the resurrection of the last day."

"Martha, I am the resurrection and the life. Do you believe this?"

"Yes, I believe that You are the Christ."

She believes. She believes. Yeah, yeah. But Lazarus is dead.

Now fast forward to the tomb site. Jesus said to remove the stone. I can see Martha's scrunched face at the command. She said, "But Lord, by this time there will be an odor, for he has been dead four days." The quiet comment having a big underscoring message. *Why would you open the tomb?*

Belief and Unbelief. Coexisting. Martha believed, but she questioned immediately when Jesus began acting. By her actions she demonstrated a questioning of her stated belief that He *is the resurrection.*

Sometimes there is a gap between what our heads know and what our hearts have the strength to cling to. Sometimes our emotions choke out what our minds know to be true. Sometimes an avalanche of pain has buried the spirit-man inside us—the one who has the faith—and that inner man is desperately trying to breathe and claw its way out while the fleshly man is standing there watching on the sidelines, completely apathetic or unsure how to help.

And we are left in the crosshairs between the two worlds.

Lord, we believe. But help our unbelief.

Journal

Day Thirty:
The Upended Life

> *Saul rose from the ground, and although his eyes were opened, he saw nothing. So they led him by the hand and brought him into Damascus. And for three days he was without sight, and neither ate nor drank. Acts 9:8-9*

An upended life. We grievers understand this principle intimately, don't we? So did Saul.

Saul ended up in Damascus—right where he had been headed. But how he ended up there and in what condition he ended up there was *nothing* like he had planned.

In the church we read the conversion story of Saul, who later became known as the Apostle Paul, as one of the greatest celebratory stories of the New Testament. God taking the persecutor and turning him into an evangelist. But imagine for a moment what Saul experienced during this time.

He wasn't a bad man, or necessarily a "sinful" man. He was a religious man; zealous for what he thought were the things of the Lord. His whole life, *literally*, had revolved around the Jewish religion. He'd been taught at the knees of the leading religious and philosophical leaders of the time. His passion grew to such an extent that he wanted to squelch what was considered at the time to be a new "Way" of Judaism. Righteous indignation on steroids.

And in one day—a few minutes, in fact—his whole life was upended. Everything he thought he knew was challenged. Everything he lived for, his future, his faith; everything that gave him status, purpose, identity, power ... was ripped from underneath him. And he came crashing down.

I can totally understand that feeling. Can't you?

And he was left in darkness. Emotionally, mentally, and ...

quite literally.

He went from being a powerful, feared, and respected religious leader, to being led by the hand like a cripple into the city to which he was headed. And he sat. For three days. In darkness.

I imagine his mind was speeding at a hundred miles an hour, processing everything he was taught, all the Scripture he knew, and trying to reconcile it to the Lord he had spoken with, whom he had previously dismissed as a heretic—not to mention ... dead.

It must have been overwhelming. This capsizing. This crash. This subjugation.

See? Saul understood keenly what it was for one's life to be turned upside down. Just as we do. When our loss and tragedy crash-landed us on a foreign beach we did not expect—when it stole our future, unraveled our faith, stripped us of our identity and purpose—we were left in our own darkness, fumbling around like the blind man Saul was.

But what I love about Saul's story was that nothing was wasted. Everything was purposed. Could Paul have been as dramatic a witness if this hadn't been his past? Would Paul have been as effective in his evangelism ministry without first having been a Pharisee, raised and drenched in Scripture and the Law and zealously persecuting those he thought threatened the Jewish way? No. Everything that was planted, even in religiosity, even in ignorant blindness, was used to make Paul who he became: a man who knew the mindset of the religious, who knew the intricacies of the Law and who could then have dramatic revelations in the Law once the Light came.

The crash doesn't have to be the end. You may feel like Saul probably did those three days—that life will never right itself, that the darkness and confusion will overtake you and that your very foundation of life has crumbled.

Don't be afraid of sitting in that darkness. Saul did. Because in the darkness, God is putting the puzzle pieces together.

Journal

Day Thirty-One:
The Great Sifting

Satan demanded to have you, that he might sift you like wheat, but I have prayed for you ... Luke 22:31-32

I don't know why, but growing up, when I heard this verse where Jesus spoke with Peter, I always stopped, right where I stopped above. "But I have prayed for you..." And somehow, in my mind, I concluded that Jesus was telling Peter, "Satan wants you. But I prayed for you. So, he's not getting you." I imagined Jesus' prayer as a blockade against Satan's quest.

It was later in life when I realized that's not at all what it was saying. Jesus said, "But I have prayed for you, *that your faith may not fail.*"

It stopped me in my tracks when I realized that Jesus was basically saying: Satan wanted to sift you, Peter, and he *will*. God granted permission. Jesus' prayer was that his faith would not fail in the midst of the sifting.

God doesn't always block the sifting. And sifting is painful. It's a separation. A forcing and cracking. A breaking open. A tearing apart. Yet we have an intercessor on our behalf. "I have prayed that your faith will not fail."

But my faith has *failed,* you might be saying. I said it too. When all we see is the lack in ourselves: the lack of hope, the lack of faith, and the lack of strength. All we feel is the bitterness and the pain.

And what's great is we see Peter's "failure" too. This is what makes this whole story so ironic—and so encouraging. Because Jesus continued and said, "I have prayed that your faith may not fail. *And when you have turned again, strengthen your brothers."*

Wait, what? It almost seems contradictory. Praying for his faith *not* to fail, yet in the same breath to acknowledge that he would turn away and have to *"turn again"* to come back.

133

Which begs the question: Did Jesus not consider it an utter failure of faith to go through a season of doubt and struggle and retreat? Because that's exactly what Peter ended up doing after Jesus' death.

Maybe even when our faith feels broken, detached, and unraveled, it really isn't a failure. If so, then Peter would have failed. And I'm pretty sure Jesus' prayers did not go ungranted. Jesus knew Peter would go through a dark valley, but He knew he would come out the other side.

The Greek word for "fail" in this verse means to leave, quit, or cease. As long as there is a shaky breath left in the lungs of your faith, as long as you're still clawing at the muck that is suffocating it, you haven't failed. Because you haven't stopped.

The Greek word for "turned again" means to return or bring back. Jesus was literally acknowledging that Peter would wander. And return. Yet He apparently did not consider that a true failure.

Friend, if you feel a failure right now … if you're feeling defeated … realize that you are reading this book, right now, so you haven't quit. You are struggling, and that's okay. You may be in that painful sifting, that excruciating cracking. There may be parts inside of you split wide open. There may be nerves exposed. There may be things breaking apart.

But Jesus whispers, "But I have prayed for you, that your faith may not fail. And when you come back, strengthen your brothers."

You have an intercessor, my friend. A powerful one.

Journal

Day Thirty-Two:
Do Something!

O LORD, how long shall I cry for help, and you will not hear?
Habakkuk 1:2

I have pointed out several times in Scriptures where someone voiced open honesty to God; questioning Him, venting to Him, even spilling anger to Him.

This is what Habakkuk the prophet did here. *O Lord, how long shall I cry for help and you will not hear? Or cry to you 'Violence!' and you will not save? Why do you make me see iniquity, and why do you idly look at wrong?* (verses 2-3)

Habakkuk is complaining about God's seeming "inaction." There was so much evil, so much terror, so much injustice and God was apparently "idle," doing nothing.

This is one of only a few times in Scripture when God literally answers someone. God responds, "I am doing a work in your days that you would not believe if told." He goes on to say how in the background, away from what Habakkuk can see, He is raising up the Chaldeans to execute justice and discipline on the nation of Judah — the very evil people Habakkuk had been complaining that God was doing nothing to stop.

First lesson: God is working in the background even when we can't see. Always. Forever. From the first day of creation until now, tomorrow, and the end of time. He has never stopped being in control.

Even after God answers, Habakkuk goes on to complain again! How brave of him. And how completely reassuring to me when I find myself doing it. God is gracious to answer again. He reminds Habakkuk that though His promise seems slow, "wait for it, it will surely come." In this second answer from God comes the famous verse, "The righteous will live by faith." It is the verse quoted not once, not twice, but *three* times in the New Testament. One of the most quoted, and one of the foundational principal truths of Scripture.

Second lesson: Faith carries us through the times when we cannot see. The very definition of faith is believing even when we can't see. That's why it's so stinking hard!

Paul made this statement in Romans 8:24, "Now hope that is seen is not hope. For who hopes for what he sees?" When there are no answers, no logic, no solutions, no awareness or understanding, it's choosing to *know* that God still is everything He said. Like a stormy sky, blanketed in grey, dark clouds, knowing the sun is still there, just hidden.

Habakkuk couldn't see God doing anything. Maybe you can't either. Yet He was. He is. We may not always like it, despise it, even. I'm pretty sure many of God's people didn't *like* the process of how He worked. Joseph thrown into a pit, becoming a slave, falsely accused, thrown into prison. Jonah, sent to an enemy nation to offer God's *forgiveness*. David spending years on the run, living as a nomad with no steady home, trying to escape the grip of the king who wanted to kill him. Jeremiah and Habakkuk and many other prophets, living lives as outcasts, ridiculed, scoffed at and sometimes beaten and killed by the people they were trying to help listen to God.

Be frustrated. Be angry. Be tired. But don't give up! Don't give in! Don't concede! The Bible says to "hold fast" many times. Why? Because we would feel like letting go many times.

Look at what Habakkuk the prophet says after his talk with God. *Though the fig tree should not blossom, nor fruit be on the vines, the produce of the olive fail and the fields yield no food ... yet I will rejoice in the LORD ... God, the Lord, is my strength.* (verses 17-19)

Ah, yes. *That's* what faith does. It carries you through. Hold tight, friend. Hold tight.

Journal

Day Thirty-Three:
The Great Wrestling

Your name shall no longer be called Jacob, but Israel, for you have striven with God and with men, and have prevailed. Genesis 32:28

Jacob fled from home as a young man after tricking his brother out of his inheritance. His brother was masculine, a hunter, probably one worth fearing. Years later, after getting married and having children, Jacob returns to his home country. Even after more than twenty years, he was afraid of facing his brother — the one he betrayed. He sent messengers ahead of him. When they came back, they told him his brother was coming to meet him ... with *four hundred men*. Yikes.

Jacob was scared out of his wits.

Sandwiched between the preparation for meeting his brother and the actual event, is a portion of Scripture where Jacob wrestles with a man. We aren't given details of how this wrestling started. But the man is revealed to be a theophany of God Himself. God appearing in angel form.

All night they wrestled. I wonder if the physical wrestling became a manifestation of Jacob's inner wrestling. You know, all that stuff on the inside working its way out. From his errant deception of his youth, to his long journey of being used by his sly father-in-law, Jacob had seen God's faithfulness and blessing — favor he *knew* he didn't deserve. And as he was on the cusp of facing his past and coming to a reckoning of where God was taking him, Jacob's inner battle must have raged.

Thus, the Great Wrestling with God. There was so much angst in him that even when God was ready to be done, Jacob wouldn't let go. "Not until you bless me," he said. In the chaotic venting of everything Jacob was processing, somewhere along the way it morphed into a need — a need to be blessed by the very one he was struggling against. Whatever Jacob sought to gain in that wrestling session, whatever questions or confusion or anger or anxiety he was trying to work out, at the end, all he really craved was God's blessing.

God changed Jacob's identity that day. Jacob … to Israel. And Israel walked away with a limp, a painful reminder of what he experienced.

The wrestling is due its season. Hear me. If your struggle is there, it must work itself out. It can't be ignored or wished away. Don't feel guilty for wrestling with God. Jacob did.

But just as the struggle is due its season, so is the cessation of it. From Jacob to Israel.

Eventually finding a new kind of contentedness should be part of healing. At some point, an acceptance. In my personal story, after all the bitterness, all the questions, all the apathy, all the fighting, there came a surrender. I became so weary of the battle. So tired of carrying the anger and confusion. I didn't know why God chose the death of my husband, but I gave up trying, or needing, to understand. And with that surrender comes a slow seeping of peace. An acceptance. The ability to move forward and focus on what to do with the rest of the days God gives here on earth, rather than be consumed with what can't be changed.

It is easy to slip into retrospect — not the healthy kind for memories — but the looking back that stirs nothing but longing and discontent and prevents one from accepting what is today.

Oh, surrender is hard. The hardest, in fact. And if you're not ready, the very idea tastes bitter. But at some point, the wrestling becomes exhausting. One day, you will long for rest. And after the fighting, the demand for answers, the quest to show God how angry you are, you will know the time has come. Time to lay down the burden. Cease the fight. And simply say, "Bless me, Lord."

God will change your identity on that day.

Journal

Day Thirty-Four:
The Nature of God

In faithfulness you have afflicted me. Let your steadfast love comfort me. Psalm 119:75-76

It's a massive thing to try to understand the nature of God. He is so much more than we are as humans. When we study Him, we realize (in our human minds) He is somehow opposites abiding in one Being. He is Love. But also Vengeance. He is Compassion. But also Justice. He dishes out grace, but asks for righteousness. He is absolutely sovereign, yet works through our free will.

These are the combinations that make Him uniquely God, uniquely *not* man, and uniquely beyond our comprehension. Isn't it glorious? There are many times in Scripture where He displays this polarity of character.

He punished the Israelites for worshipping a golden calf after He delivered them from Egypt. Yet during their forty years of punishment to wander the desert, their shoes never wore out, their clothing never deteriorated, their food never failed to arrive and His guidance (a.k.a. the pillar of cloud and fire) never left. You see? Just and Compassionate, at the same time.

Now back to our verse up top. David recognized two things. God allowed the affliction. God was faithful. Both are true. At the same time. (It stings a little, doesn't it?) That's hard for us to comprehend. He allows heartache. Yet He never stops being a God working in our lives, willing to bear the load and heal our broken souls. He allows tragedy. But He never stops giving of Himself to our weakened state.

It's kind of like how He allowed Joseph to be betrayed by his own family and sold as a slave. A teenager, thrust into an unknown world, dropped into a foreign land. He went from being a beloved son, to being the pit of society. He didn't know their ways, didn't know their culture, he didn't even know their language. Can you imagine the shock? Yet it says in Scripture that God's favor was with Joseph. Then God allowed him to be falsely accused, bearing a punishment for a crime he didn't even commit. Year after year, he waited for justice in prison. But God's favor still rested upon him. God allowed it all. And yet, God's favor followed him wherever he went, from the moment he was betrayed by his brothers. Slavery and God's favor? Prison and God's favor? Coexisting? What?

Funny little thought, huh?

In our bitterness and hurt, sometimes it's a little too easy for us to agree with the "He allowed this affliction" and not give adequate agreement to the "faithfulness" part. I remember singing a song in church: "You have been so, so good to me" was one of the lines. (*Reckless Love*, by Caleb Culver, Cory Asbury and Ran Jackson. Richmond Park Publishing, copyright 2018) And I remember struggling singing that line with sincerity. Has He really been good? *So, so* good? It didn't feel like it. My heart kind of grumbled its doubt.

So then, the question is our definition of good. Is He good because He never allowed the bad to touch us? Or is He good because He never leaves us even when the bad *is* touching us?

David went on to discuss his experience during affliction. "If your word had not been my delight, I would have perished in my affliction." (Ps. 119:92) The truth of the matter is affliction does have the power to take you down if you let it. But God's Word is the rock, remember. Unmovable. Unchanging. So we hold on to His Word. We clasp it, knowing it is the buoy in the flood. Knowing the truths within are the things that can combat the emotional tidal waves that lie to our hearts and blind our souls. Knowing the truths within are the things that lead us back after we are lost. Knowing the truths within are a "lamp to my feet and a light to my path." (Verse 105)

"This is my comfort in my affliction, that your promise gives me life." (Verse 50)

Journal

Day Thirty-Five:
The Lord Has Dealt Bitterly

And the women said, "Is this Naomi?" She said to them, "Do not call me Naomi; call me Mara, for the Almighty has dealt very bitterly with me. I went away full and the LORD has brought me back empty." Ruth 1:19-21

Oh, Naomi. We feel you. *Don't call me blessed. I am left in ashes. My life is gone.*

Naomi had to deal with three blows of grief. The death of her husband and the death of both her grown sons. Ouch! No wonder she struggled. Poor Naomi. She's older. What could life possibly have for her to look forward to?

Well, in her case, it was the love of a daughter-in-law. The act of helping Ruth, helped Naomi. And when Ruth was able to marry their kinsman-redeemer, a baby was born. And in chapter 4 of Ruth, the mood of the story changed. And so did the mood of Naomi. "Then the women said to Naomi, 'Blessed be the Lord, who has not left you this day without a redeemer … He shall be to you a restorer of life and a nourisher of your old age, for your daughter-in-law who loves you, who is more to you than seven sons, has given birth to him.'" (Verses 14-15)

That child changed the course of Naomi's life, her perspective, but also history. It goes on to say that baby's name was Obed, the "father of Jesse, the father of David."

It's easy to read someone else's biography and see how God's hand was upon the trials. It's easy to read the end of their story and see that God had not forsaken them but actually had a plan the entire time. Do you realize if Naomi had not lost her husband and both sons, she would have never returned to Bethlehem? Ruth would have never met Boaz. Obed would never have been born, which means Jesse wouldn't have been born, King David would never have been born, and eventually our Messiah, who was born of that lineage. Actually, the *entire* history of Israel would have looked different. And possibly the world. Whoa…

Did Naomi have any clue of the plan God had? Nope. She was just bitter.

And honestly, when you're bitter, the promise that God has a plan doesn't actually make you feel better. At least it didn't for me. (I'm not the only one, right?) I didn't want to hear how God was going to work through the death of my husband. Why couldn't He have worked through his life, instead? I didn't want to ponder what God would accomplish through my tragedy. I didn't want to think about how He works all things for the good. I was just bitter.

God's redemption is rarely what we envisioned. Naomi lost her sons. The redemption was giving her a grandson. Yet for her, that baby was a token of God's grace.

Nothing is wasted with God. Of course, it's easier to spout all this when tragedy hasn't touched you. Quite a bit harder when it has. But do you believe it to be true? Can you take a weak, failing, embittered hand and reach for that sliver of truth?

Grief forces changes. Changes unfold different life paths. Different life paths create different opportunities, different choices, different meetings, different relationships and different outcomes. We yearn for what was. Understandably. But have you thought about the fact that these life changes will take you to experience totally different things, meet totally different people and possibly influence totally different lives?

It's okay to be bitter. But you don't have to stay there. She *was* Mara—bitter. But she morphed again and became Naomi—blessed. I have met people and formed new dreams that would have never been birthed without my husband's death. Does that mean I'm glad my husband died and I was thrust onto a new life journey? Of course not.

But being at peace with what you can't change is part of healing.

Journal

Day Thirty-Six:
When You Feel Spiritually Dead

He [God] brought me out in the Spirit ... and set me down in the middle of the valley; it was full of bones ... they were very dry. And he said to me, "Son of man, can these bones live?"
Ezekiel 37:1-3

Resurrection.

The first thing that probably comes to mind is a dead body returning to life. But there is more to the concept of resurrection than just physical. Resurrection of hope. Resurrection of joy. Resurrection of peace. Resurrection of purpose. Resurrection of passion.

And for resurrection to happen, it means death has happened.

Death. Such a dark word. *Death has happened.*

With the death of a loved one, we often have portions of ourselves that die with them. Death of our plans. Death of our expected future. Death of our trust in God's sovereignty or love. Death of the consistency of our faith.

God is in the business of resurrection. Because, unfortunately, death is part of our world. Part of humanity. And the physical death of a loved one often ripples into other forms of death in the lives of those left behind.

Ezekiel could have simply stated that he stood in a valley full of bones. But he added the words, "they were very dry." Why? It tells us that the death he was seeing was death that had been in place for a while. It wasn't fresh or recent. They weren't still in the process of decaying. These corpses were bones without a speck of tissue or flesh. They were *dry.*

But then God asked the prophet a crazy, unthinkable question. "Can these bones live?"

I can imagine Ezekiel biting his tongue for some sarcastic comment that wanted to spill. Or maybe that's just me projecting my own bitter sarcasm. Like, really, Lord? Can they live? They're bones. They're dead. They're done. They've been that way for a while.

But then God said to Ezekiel, "Prophesy over these bones." (Eze. 37:4) Gulp. You know when God gives a command it's because He has a plan. What could God do with a valley of death? What could He do with dry bones that are but a memory of the vitality that once lived there?

Oh, that's right. He is the God of resurrection.

When we feel spiritually dry—spiritually dead—we can remember that God has the power to resurrect. We don't have to make it happen. We don't have to rush it. We simply need to allow God to work. And maybe even once in a while, prophesy to ourselves.

God spoke again to Ezekiel. "They say, 'Our bones are dried up, and our hope is lost; we are indeed cut off.'" Do you feel that way? Your hope feels lost. You're dried up. Your faith, your life, is cut off from the life that once was there.

Listen to God's voice: "Thus says the Lord God; Behold I will open your graves and raise you from your graves, O my people ... And you shall know that I am the Lord, when I open your graves." (Eze. 37: 12)

He's speaking promises of resurrection. Rebirth. Renaissance.

The promises of God need not make you feel all gooey inside. But they can remind you that life is more than what you feel right now. Understand that God knows that these spiritual and emotional deaths are part of our human existence. We are but dust. He knows our frailties.

That's why He reminds us what business He is in.

Journal

Day Thirty-Seven:
As One Gone Astray

If a man has a hundred sheep, and one of them has gone astray, does he not leave the ninety-nine on the mountains and go in search of the one that went astray? Matthew 18:12

It's interesting. This parable is found twice in the gospels. But the scenario behind each is different. In Luke, they are specifically talking about sinners. In Matthew, they've asked who is the greatest in the kingdom and Jesus brings a little child over and starts giving a lesson. This parable, of leaving the ninety-nine, is included in the lesson. He concludes by saying it isn't the Father's will that any of these little ones should perish.

The heart of the story? Each person is valuable. Each person is one the Father desires. Even the lowly and the outcast.

What's interesting about this parable is that it came alive to me after grief. I grew up in church, always thinking of the prodigal sons and daughters who had wandered in sin and when they "come back," the Lord and the church celebrate their return. This is the context in Luke's telling of the parable.

But after my loss, I didn't wander away in sin. I didn't "backslide" in the traditional thinking of the word. I didn't stop going to church, or start living in open sin, or change my lifestyle to one of drunkenness or debauchery. But my heart was far away, nonetheless.

Open sin isn't the only version of a heart that has wandered.

It's not just the people who drift into immorality, rebelliousness and prodigal living that Jesus comes after. It's even the people who have wandered away in grief, disillusionment, anger, and hurt. These are things that, like a little sheep wandering in the remote mountains, can lure you far away from the pasture where the Shepherd is keeping watch.

Grief, disillusionment, anger, and apathy are all as potent as open sin and rebellion. They are just as effective in distancing us from God. They are just as strong of a lure, causing us to, step by step, veer and stray and stumble until we look around and see we are so far away from where we should be.

We are still that One. The One in the story.

And He still comes to find us.

When I say this parable came alive to me, it was this revelation that spurred it. As I struggled with my position in my faith — one of distance — I knew God would have to come find me. Come woo me. Come shepherd me.

And He did. Time after time He did something to provide, to speak, to encourage, to challenge or to remind me. I wish I could say I "felt" His comfort in those early days. But I really didn't. In my numbness I think I was immune to it. Which is why He had to woo me and work to draw me back. Which is why this parable stood out to me. For the first time in my life, I saw myself as that One. The One He pursued. The One He came to find. The One He put effort into bringing back. It's not just the sinner who walked from his life of faith whom this story personifies, it's also us: The Grievers. The ones whose pain, anger and hurt have put a mountain range between us and our Shepherd.

Fear not. Your Shepherd will come for you. Expect it. Look for it. And relish in it.

Journal

Day Thirty-Eight:
The Condemning Heart

For whenever our heart condemns us, God is greater than our heart, and he knows everything. 1 John 3:20

A little verse. But, oh, so weighted. Has your heart ever condemned you?

Grief often has lots of guilt mixed in. Guilt sneaks up in various forms and shades. It is sometimes produced by uncontrolled forces in which we have no say, and other times it is our own choices that bring it to a head. The power of guilt, whether external or internal, illogical or logical, is a force as powerful and unpredictable as grief itself. It makes the grief journey complicated and hard to understand. Sometimes we can bear the weight of sadness, but guilt has power to twist and manipulate us.

Guilt for being alive when they're not. Guilt for all the things you regret or all the what-ifs that pound your brain—and none of it can you change. Guilt for something as simple as smiling. Sometimes we are caught in a vortex ... pulled to keep living ... pulled to move out of the depression ... while being sucked into the need to feel loyal to the grief. This guilt can be the hardest to balance. The hardest to understand.

Guilt for succeeding without them or the thought of becoming happy without them. Guilt for how you've handled yourself, the situation, relationships, and even ... your faith. Guilt for what you've had to do, maybe with their possessions, with the dreams and plans or with the things that represented them. Guilt for failing people's expectations or even your loved one's memory. Guilt for your doubts, anger, and resentment. Guilt that you're struggling so badly and can't shake it.

"Heart" is a term that symbolizes our emotions, senses and

161

mental capacity. We often know that our emotions can lead us astray. Even the book of Jeremiah tells us, "The heart is deceitful above all things." (Jer. 17:9) So why do we let those feelings of guilt define us so much?

There is something awe-inspiring about the simple truth that what we feel isn't necessarily true. Something encouraging to know we don't necessarily need to give credence to all the thoughts that jumble our brains.

When our heart is condemning us, we can trust that God is bigger than that. We can remind ourselves of the truth.

The last four words of the verse above offer even more awe-inspiring encouragement. God knows. Everything. Even in our darkest moments, our desperate moments, our grief-stricken moments, He sees it all. He knows all the tumultuous craziness. He understands all the doubts and misgivings, questions and anger. And even with all that knowledge, His truth stands.

His. Truth. Stands. What is that truth? *"When our heart condemns us, God is greater than our heart."*

Remember the old hymn, "Leaning on the Everlasting Arms"? What beautiful imagery. We have arms to lean on. Arms that aren't too short to save, or too weak to raise, or too tired to carry. We have access to the Everlasting Arms.

Which means Everlasting Hope.

Journal

Day Thirty-Nine:
The God Who Sees

Let us then with confidence draw near to the throne of grace,
that we may receive mercy and find grace to help in time of need.
Hebrews 4:16

Confidence. Let us *come*. With *confidence*. To *His throne*. To receive *mercy* and *help* in our time of need. Why? Because He understands.

The verse right before this in Hebrews 4 tells us that we have a high priest, Jesus, who can sympathize with our weaknesses, because He experienced the pressure of being *tempted*, meaning "put to the test." He understands the weight of the struggle. And, not just being tempted to sin, our high priest even knows what it is to *feel* abandoned. In Matthew 27:46, on the cross, He cries out, "My God, My God, why have you forsaken me?" echoing the words in Psalm 22 of David who felt the same sensation.

Have you ever thought about why God so often in Scripture tells us not to be afraid? Maybe it's because we often *feel* the fear. Why does God speak of His faithfulness over and over? Maybe because we would question it, over and over. Ever wonder why He reminds us throughout the Scriptures that He will be with us? Never leave us? Maybe it's because we will often *feel* forsaken.

Job said in 29:2-4, "Oh that I were as in the months of old, as in the days when God watched over me, when his lamp shone upon my head ... when the friendship of God was upon my tent." Ah, the days of old. Back when he didn't feel like God had forsaken him.

Isn't that so relatable? If you feel like that today, know that you have an intercessor, a high priest, and a Savior, who knows that feeling intimately. And know that you have a God who reminds us consistently of the truth of His presence.

165

I'm reminded of the story of Hagar in Genesis. After being given to Abraham to bear a child, after conceiving and having tension come between her and her mistress, Sara, Hagar ran away. She didn't have family to rush back to, or a town to find refuge in. She was in the wilderness. Alone. Estranged. Hopeless. The angel of the Lord found her in that remote place and spoke with her. The angel promised the son within her would become a mighty man and form a mighty nation.

Oh, how we need promises in those desperate times.

Then the angel said she would name her son Ishmael, which means *God Hears,* because, the angel said, *God has listened to your affliction.* Wow. Imagine in your most desperate moments having those words spoken to you.

Good news. You have. Right this minute.

Hagar called the Lord who spoke to her, *"You are the God who sees me."* How wonderful, how personal, how intimate, how glorious is that? That moment when you realize the God of all creation ... sees ... *you*. Hears ... *you*. Acknowledges ... *you*. Has compassion on ... *you*.

I can only imagine Hagar's soul reviving. After going from slave, to mistress, to pregnant, to reviled, to a runaway. She probably struggled knowing who she was, where she belonged, what she wanted or what her status should be. Confused to the core. In all the chaos of wild emotions and high tempers, she sat by a brook in the wilderness, away from anyone, and Someone found her. The God Who Sees.

My God. Your God. The same God who promised to be with us, to never forsake us.

This is the hope we have. Remember the reminder later in Hebrews: "We have this as a sure and steadfast anchor of the soul." Oh, thank God for an anchor to hold us steady in the storm. An anchor that is sure and dependable.

Journal

Day Forty:
At the Scent of Water

For there is hope for a tree, if it be cut down, that it will sprout again ... Job 14:7

When my husband died, with all the chaos that was inside me, I remember trying to explain to myself what I felt. I needed to put it into words, into a visual that would make sense. Something I could even tell others that could metaphorically summarize my sensation. One day it came to me. I said, "I feel like a tree, completely cut down." That word picture made sense. Everything that was my life, was gone. A chainsaw had come and razed the life we built. I felt dead. Broken. Lost. Only a stump remaining.

It wasn't but a few days after verbalizing my feelings into this word picture that I came across the above verse in Job. It was one of those moments—you know, *those* moments—when it's like God *literally* responded to me.

Me: *looking up at the sky* Really, God?

God: *nodding*

It gave me chill bumps that first time I read it because it was so direct, so precise, so specific to what I had verbalized that I knew God spoke to me. Job wrote that verse, not knowing thousands of years later, a young widow would cry out to God, frustrated and broken, and God would use his words to cut through her depression and speak hope.

And He partnered it with a memory. You see, when my husband and I bought our property, there were eucalyptus trees everywhere, some being fifty feet tall. Others, you could tell had grown naturally from seeds through the years. They were smaller and not manicured with one main trunk like the bigger ones.

The problem? They were messy. All. The. Time.

My husband got in his mind that he would, one by one, cut

169

them down to rid ourselves of the mess. He started with the smaller ones he could handle himself without a professional tree service. One weekend he chopped a few down, leaving only stumps behind. Taken care of, right?

Little did we know, those stumps, left to themselves, would grow again. Sprouts formed. Little, wild branches grew. Leaves flourished. Soon, it looked like massive bushes from those "dead" stumps.

When I read this verse in Job that day, God brought to mind that time, about eight years earlier. He reminded me of a blessed truth: Even after being cut down, I can grow again—just like my eucalyptus trees.

If we hadn't taken further steps on those stumps, those eucalyptus trees would have continued to grow, wild and unchecked, even after devastation. Of course, they would have never looked like their previous form, no. That's not possible. They would have looked completely different. But they were alive and growing. Even being cut down hadn't stopped them.

It's hard to think of "thriving" after heartbreak. It feels disloyal. But did you know one of the definitions of "thrive" is simply to grow? If you can only handle one goal, let it simply be to grow. Grow deeper. Grow more thoughtful. More thankful. More compassionate. More hopeful. Try to be willing to step out of your comfort zone and open yourself up to possibilities.

After grief, we need reminding of this same truth. Our life will never look the same after being cut down. That's hard to accept for quite a while. But this verse in Job goes on to say, "Yet at the scent of water it will bud." Ah. I love that. *At the scent.* The water hasn't even come yet, but the scent lets us know the water's coming. Can you smell the rain? Smell the hope? Smell the promise?

Journal

ABOUT THE AUTHOR

Alisha had served in various ministry capacities for twenty years, when she was thrown into widowhood at age thirty-three. She fought the battle of grieving well, learning deep lessons of life, faith, and suffering. Bringing grief, tragedy, and the fight for hope into writing, both fiction and nonfiction, became her calling.

She blogs on her website, *alishabozarth.com*, where she delves into the tough subjects of loss, the struggle of faith, and digging for hope. Four blogs have been featured in national grief newsletters, with others listed on online resource sites. Her blog "Widowhood is More Than..." has gone viral with thousands of views and shares.

Alisha resides in Bakersfield, California, where she homeschools her two high school daughters, and upkeeps her two acres (but not very well! It's a lot of work!) and writes to illustrate that *Hope Grows in the Wilderness*. A lover of coffee, chocolate and pastries, and (so she doesn't sound too fat) a lover of God, history and traveling. When she can, she travels to fulfill her bucket list of seeing all fifty states, and hopefully, eventually, other countries.